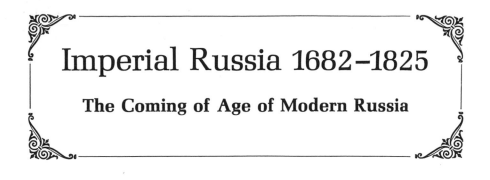

Imperial Russia 1682–1825

The Coming of Age of Modern Russia

Borzoi History of Russia

VOLUME 4

General Editor:

MICHAEL CHERNIAVSKY
State University of New York at Albany

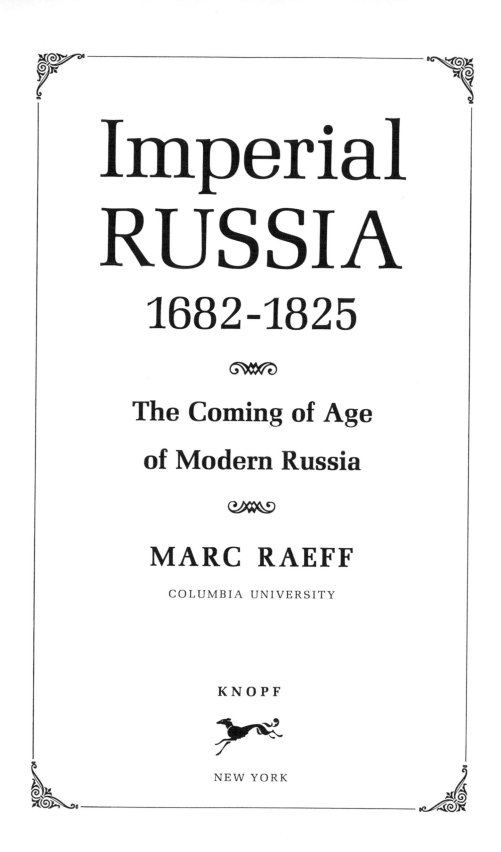

Imperial
RUSSIA
1682-1825

The Coming of Age
of Modern Russia

MARC RAEFF

COLUMBIA UNIVERSITY

KNOPF

NEW YORK

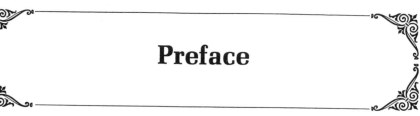

Preface

This is volume four of a six volume history of Russia. The publication of Russian history in six volumes presents certain obvious technical advantages—size, selection, and distribution. But all this is secondary: the chief justification for this format was the need to overcome the main fault of general histories —the attempt, on the part of one historian, to cover the whole span of a complex and very long process within a very large society. Hence, each volume is written by the best available expert in the particular period of concentration; in the case of this volume on eighteenth-century Russia, Professor Marc Raeff of Columbia University is the recognized authority in the field not only outside but even inside the Soviet Union.

The choice of the number—six—however, is not accidental or random. It presupposes a legitimacy of division, of periodization, which is the main justification and subject of this preface. The problem lies in the fact that periodization is both necessary and provocative by definition. It indicates our recognition that there are both continuities and changes to be discerned in the historical process; at moments when the discontinuities and changes seem to outweigh the continuances and the familiar, we establish breaking points, the beginning of one period and the culmination of another. Insofar as historians agree on these moments, periodization is useful and even necessary, allowing a common language and the use of characterizations which are understood by all historians. Yet periodization is provocative, for it is based on subjective judgment (no matter how widely accepted) as to what changed and what continued, what aspect of the historical process is important and which one is minor.

The Russian eighteenth century with which this volume is largely concerned is as challenging in its periodization as any other period of Russian history. Professor Raeff appears to follow traditional

historiography when he begins the period with the reforms of Peter
the Great. The generally accepted argument is that these reforms
transformed Russia from an "eastern" medieval society into a backward but even more westernized European power, from Muscovy
into the Russian Empire. But Raeff ends this volume at 1825, with
the death of Alexander I, after the Napoleonic wars rather than with
the convenient date of 1801 which marked the murder of the
Emperor Paul I. Thereby Raeff challenges one of the accepted characteristics of traditional historiography which saw the eighteenth
century as the period of "gentry monarchy," expressed most dramatically in the raising and deposition (and murder) of rulers by
young officers of the guards regiments, members of the gentry,
whose last successful action was the murder of Paul I. Hence, by a
shift of twenty-four years, Raeff rejects the concept of "gentry monarchy" in favor of describing a process of bureacratization and
rationalization of government which comes to some kind of fruition
by 1825.

Of course, one can argue with Raeff. One can argue that the
reforms of Peter the Great, for instance, marked no significant
change from the seventeenth century, that "westernization" is a
misleading abstraction, that the reality of adoption of "western"
ideas and things existed since the sixteenth century, and that the
"westernization" under Peter the Great differed from the preceding
age largely because of the growing xenophobia of the Russian masses
and the particular crudeness of Peter's methods. Or, one can argue
that the image of a new society, a new Russia created by Peter, is
contradicted or modified strongly by the fact that the Russian ruling
class, the aristocracy of the eighteenth century, is the same as it was
a century earlier; or one can argue, based on economic data, that
the intellectual and social westernization of the Russian nobility
was, in fact, restricted to an extraordinarily small group which had
the means to afford the new culture, while the mass of the Russian
gentry lived more like their peasants than like their aristocratic
superiors. One can defend the idea of gentry monarchy by emphasizing all the legislation which gave the gentry a monopoly of
economic, political, and social power, or one can emphasize the
predominance of French Enlightenment in Russia over German
philosophy by dwelling on the style of the court rather than on the
writings of intellectuals. One may argue all these positions largely
because they are to varying degrees true, depending upon how
important we judge particular aspects of society. We may also be
assured that these arguments shall go on as long as history is being
written. But to say that we can argue against any or all of Raeff's
positions is also to say that he presents us with a powerful and

reasoned conception of Russian history in this particular period—
so well reasoned, so consistent, and so powerful that it is imposing,
and yet challenges us, hopefully, to argue and to think.

Albany, New York   **Michael Cherniavsky**
                                                        General Editor

Acknowledgments

T hough this is volume four of the history, it is the first one to be published. Hence, I can find no better opportunity or place to express my gratitude and admiration for my friend, William Frohlich, until recently the history editor at the Random House/Alfred A. Knopf college department. The format and the very conception of this multivolume history were his. His was the prodding that drove me to undertake the task of editing this history; his, the patience with my complaints, unreliability, and unreasonable demands; and his, the intellectual discrimination that allowed for no compromises and demanded the best from the authors and from the editor.

Still, this would not suffice if this volume (and hopefully all the forthcoming volumes of the history) had not received the benefit of the extraordinary editorial skill of Lynne Farber of Random House. The editor and the author can only thank her for a superb job.

M.C.

June 1970

Contents

xi

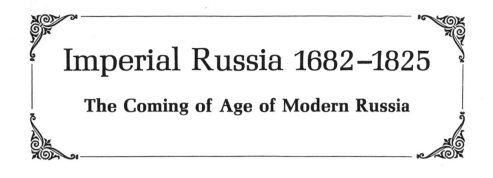

Imperial Russia 1682–1825

The Coming of Age of Modern Russia

Political Chronicle

On April 27, 1682, the Great Lord and Tsar of All Russia, Feodor Alekseevich, died. In line to succeed him were two boys, his brother, Ivan, sickly and retarded, and Peter, his half-brother, only ten years old. With the assistance of the semiprofessional musketeers (streltsy) garrisoned in Moscow, the energetic sister of Feodor, Sophie, seized power and declared herself regent, proclaiming both Ivan and Peter co-tsars. Because she was in conflict with the family of Peter's mother, the Naryshkins, Sophie forced the boy to reside on one of the suburban estates of the crown.

The young co-Tsar Peter grew up away from the constricting atmosphere of the Kremlin, largely left to his own devices under his mother's lax supervision. Lively and energetic, the youngster became passionately fond of military things; after discovering a boat (made "lake-worthy" by a Dutch carpenter), he also became an enthusiastic sailor. For his war games, he enlisted the children of domestics as well as the sons of his mother's courtiers. With the help of older service nobles and under the guidance of foreigners who resided in the Foreign Quarter, Peter organized his own "play regiments." In 1689 these proved strong enough to challenge the regent and bring about her downfall. Yet even then Peter did not take over the reins of government, letting his mother and her family do the ruling while he continued to sail his boat, to organize war games, and to associate with the foreign residents of Moscow. He was fascinated by the way of life he observed in the Foreign Quarter and participated in it with great zest. He seems to have been attracted most by the greater freedom—bodily, social, sexual, and intellectual—he enjoyed in the company of foreigners; he also found recognition for his own drive and energy among the ambitious and adventurous foreigners who had come to seek their fortunes in Russia.

Peter was curious and alert, and eager to learn. He spent the years between 1689 and 1696 in the company of foreigners acquiring mechanical skills and accumulating as much knowledge as he could. At the same time, he was reorganizing his military establishment on the Western model, using his "play regiments" (soon to be transformed into regiments of the Guards) as test models. He hoped to lead this improved military force in defeating Russia's traditional enemy, the Turks. On the death of his mother in 1696 he took over the actual governance of his realm. (His sickly coruler, Ivan, incapable of anything except to sit silently at official ceremonies, died soon thereafter anyway.)

It is important to remember that the main focus of Peter's early activities was military. He wanted to succeed where his predecessors had failed—to secure the southern frontier of the state. He may possibly also have had a more or less conscious desire to realize the dream of Orthodox churchmen and free Constantinople from the infidels. His first move was a campaign to capture Azov, which failed primarily because he could not blockade the city from the sea. Undaunted and displaying for the first time the tenacity that was to be so characteristic of his rule, he set out to build a navy and to equip his army anew. The following year, 1697, he laid siege to Azov again; this time his small navy succeeded in blockading the fortress effectively from the sea and brought about its capitulation. The tsar's triumphant return to Moscow was made a public display in the neoclassical taste.

The second goal in Peter's immediate program combined an educational trip abroad with the organization of an anti-Turkish crusade of European Christian powers. In August 1697 Peter left for a lengthy journey to the West, the first Russian ruler to do so. His appearance created quite a sensation in the countries he passed through, particularly in the small German principalities. After he had reached Holland, he isolated himself from his retinue and spent several months improving his knowledge of shipbuilding and navigation. He then crossed over to England to continue his naval apprenticeship. He ordered young sons of the nobility to follow his example, and many were sent abroad to study and acquire Western naval techniques. He also engaged the services of foreign technicians and purchased scientific instruments, books, and curiosities that were shipped back home, where they served to launch museums, laboratories, and libraries. Considering the short time he spent in the West, Peter was remarkably successful in furthering his own knowledge and in laying the groundwork for regular technical and intellectual exchanges. But he failed in his diplomatic efforts to bring about an anti-Turkish coalition. In the course of his negotiations with the king of Poland, however, the idea was broached of an anti-Swedish coalition (which would also include Denmark) to secure the northern flank of the three Eastern powers. The possibility of common action against Turkey afterward was left open. Successfully concluded after Peter's return to Moscow, these negotiations radically changed the orientation of the tsar's foreign policy and determined the course of his entire reign, as well as the fate of the Russian Empire for generations to come. But before turning to this momentous subject, let us briefly glance at Peter's actions upon his return to Moscow.

Peter hastened home at the news of a revolt among the *streltsy*. The revolt was effectively and ruthlessly put down by Prince F. Iu. Romodanovsky, the tsar's lieutenant in Moscow, but Peter decided to make an example of the *streltsy*, the hated symbol of Muscovite political instability and of his own past insecurity. He disbanded the corps of *streltsy* and had hundreds of them tortured and executed (allegedly he wielded the ax himself on Red Square). Quite likely the revolt confirmed him in his determination to make a clean break with the old forms of Muscovite life. In any event, after his return from Western Europe, Peter proceeded to impose Western (German) clothing and manners on his subjects, naturally first on members of the service class. His decrees concerning the wearing of European garb, the shaving of beards, the organizing of *soirées* in private homes, the smoking of tobacco, the end of women's confinement in their own quarters *(terem)*, and the substitution of coffee for tea may strike the modern reader as a bit childish and ludicrous. But for Peter they also had great symbolic significance. They meant not so much the break with the past, as the creation of a new type of Russian man. (Of course, Peter's decrees affected only the upper classes; the peasants were allowed to retain their traditional costume and hair growth.) The new Russian was to be an active, dynamic, creative individual, dedicated to serving his tsar and his country. It was to be expected that these measures would meet with resistance, especially on the part of members of the older generation who could not change their ways: Peter's more sanguine expectations of transforming Russian society overnight failed to materialize. Nonetheless, it is remarkable that within less than a generation the Russian nobility had totally abandoned both old attire and traditional ways. At least outwardly, they had become fully Westernized. And as a matter of fact, the younger people adopted the new ways with enthusiasm, for they led to a welcome freeing of social intercourse. They took advantage of the new opportunities with such zest that at the death of Peter and the accession of Catherine I, the court of St. Petersburg had become one of the gayest in all Europe.

The war with Sweden started in 1700 with a resounding defeat administered by young King Charles XII to Peter at Narva. For a while, the situation looked desperate; Peter had lost his best troops and most of his artillery. But as usual, he redoubled his energies in the face of adversity, and while Charles was bogged down in Poland in a vain attempt at imposing his candidate for the throne of the Commonwealth, Peter patiently rebuilt his army, and equipment, and trained an effective officer corps. When Charles again turned his attention to Russia and invaded the Ukraine, Peter was ready. In July 1709 at the Battle of Poltava, Charles XII was decisively defeated and barely escaped into Turkish territory with a small retinue. Peter, it is true, in pursuit of Charles let himself be trapped by the Turks on the Pruth River, but he succeeded in buying himself free at the price of an onerous treaty by which he relinquished Azov. The war against Sweden dragged on for many more years, although its eventual outcome was no longer in doubt. Peter conquered the Swedish possessions on the eastern shores of the Baltic Sea and on the Gulf of Finland, where he had laid the foundations of his new capital, St. Petersburg, in 1703; he also built a seaworthy navy in the Baltic which gave the *coup de grâce* to Sweden in 1720 and forced her into signing the Treaty of Nystad (1721). By the terms of the treaty, Peter kept most of his conquests and consolidated Russia's position as the strongest power on the shores of the Baltic. Before his death Peter waged a successful campaign against Persia that yielded significant territorial gains in the Caucasus and along the Caspian Sea.

As important as the territorial acquisitions were the political gains: Russia emerged as a major European power. In fact, Peter's successes threw the Western capitals, especially Paris and Vienna, into consternation. It was generally feared that Russia would continue her westward advance into Central Europe and upset the European balance of power. Pique as well as distrust explain Austria's refusal to acknowledge the new title of emperor that Peter's Senate had bestowed upon him in 1721; and French support of Sweden and King Stanislas Leszynski of Poland led to the regent's rejection of a matrimonial alliance with the half-barbarian despot of the East. But despite the opposition of France and Austria, Peter secured the alliance of other powers, in particular Holland, England, Brandenburg, and several other German principalities, and maintained a long-standing friendship with King Augustus of Saxony and Poland. From that time on, the Russian Empire was to be bound by matrimonial ties to numerous German principalities (for example, Holstein, Oldenburg, Mecklenburg, Baden, Württemberg). Because of the nature of the diplomatic game in the eighteenth century, Russia too became involved in all major European conflicts, shifts and reversals of alliances. In short, as a result of Peter's victories, the Russian Empire had become a permanent and significant member of the

Peter in official glory—1717

European community of states; it would never be ignored in the future.

In the process of mobilizing the resources of the country and organizing and leading his armies to victory, Peter discovered that the old framework of Muscovite government was not adequate to the task and that he had to transform the entire administrative structure of the state. At first on an ad hoc basis, later in more systematic fashion (although Peter remained a pragmatist to the last), a new government structure was erected; as a corollary, the economic and social life of the nation was significantly changed. Very briefly, Peter organized the central administration along functional lines, each aspect of it to be taken care of by a specific College (board). The operating procedures of all colleges were set by uniform

Creation of Senate

rational and bureaucratic regulations. Since Peter himself was such an energetic leader, coordination of action among the colleges as well as general planning of policy were left to chance. But because rulers of his caliber might not always appear in the future, the tsar set up the Senate as a special coordinating and planning council that would act for him during his absences from the capital as well. A network of agents, *fiskaly,* and the procurator-general of the Senate (with his staff) had the task of overseeing the implementation of policy decisions. The Russian Church, whose head, the patriarch, had at times claimed a status of near equality with the tsar, was thoroughly reorganized. After the death of Patriarch Adrian in 1700, his see was not filled, and in 1721 the Church was also given a collegial form of administration. The Holy Synod, consisting of several bishops, abbots, and priests, was put in charge of all Church matters and ecclesiastical justice. It was assisted by a chancery whose head, the *Ober-Prokurator,* a layman, in fact became the secular overseer of the Church.[1]

On the local level, Peter's efforts at reform did not work out satisfactorily. He turned his attention to this area of administration only as an afterthought, to make sure that all the human and fiscal resources needed for the war effort were adequately mobilized and accounted for. For a time, he had army regiments and their officers perform the duties of local administrative bodies. Peter also failed to provide the basic elements of self-government on which his new provincial administration, patterned on the Swedish and Baltic models, was founded. Local administration remained a weak spot in Russian public life well into the late eighteenth century, when Catherine II provided a solid framework that lasted until the zemstvo reforms of 1864. The same may be said of the reorganization of municipal government. Peter tried to introduce into Russian towns a corporative municipal self-government of a Western European type (*ratusha* and *magistrat*). But because he subordinated the organs of urban self-administration to the fiscal and police needs of the state, no genuine municipal corporations or effective self-government could take root. As a matter of fact, the heavy taxes and onerous services imposed on the municipal institutions and their elected members not only seriously handicapped the development of a strong bourgeoisie, but also ruined the average townspeople and traders.

Mobilization of the nation's resources meant, first of all, effective taxation. In imitation of practices prevailing at the time in the West, Peter introduced a number of regalias and imposed heavy indirect taxes on consumer articles such as salt and alcohol. The share of

---

[1] The organization of the judiciary is too complex and technical a subject to be dealt with here.

indirect taxes in the total revenue of the state grew apace, both in his own reign and that of his successors; eventually they came to account for more than 50 percent of the revenue. Naturally, this fiscal burden lay most heavily on the poorest consumers—the peasantry. Other forms of economic mobilization, such as tariffs, promotion of industry, and mining enterprises, will be discussed in a later chapter, but the change in the system of direct taxation must be noted here, for it had important and lasting effects on Russia's social structure. The traditional unit of direct taxation had been the peasant household, regardless of the number of able-bodied workers or families it contained. This meant, of course, that the tax revenue did not reflect the growth in population or the increase in agricultural productivity. Toward the end of his reign (about 1718), Peter established the capitation, a fixed tax on every (male) "soul"—exclusive of infants—wherever he lived or worked. By becoming himself a unit of taxation, the serf was separated from the land he tilled. From the state's point of view, he had become a movable object of taxation. The capitation therefore became the basis for the transformation of the land-bound peasant serf into chattel: at their master's will, serfs could be sold, exchanged, transferred, separated from their families and land. In fact, if not in law, the traditional serf tied to the land became a virtual slave.

The peasantry and urban dwellers were not alone in having their condition changed by Peter's military needs and administrative reforms. To staff the modernized military establishment and administration, Peter needed many officers and officials. Naturally, he turned to the nobility, whose members were put into the strait jacket of regular, permanent, and lifelong service. The Table of Ranks (1722) provided for an orderly system of advancement which opened the highest echelons of the service even to those of lowly birth. Peter also endeavored to secure the economic position of the members of the service class by forbidding the splintering of their estates among several heirs, as had been traditional. The decree on single inheritance of 1714 provided that an estate could be inherited undivided by only one son (the father having the right to designate which of his sons would be the heir); the other siblings were to be compensated in cash or movables. The nobility strongly resisted this innovation, and it had to be abrogated in 1734.

To ensure that his work of reform was carried on—or at any rate not undone by incapable heirs or vengeful traditionalists—Peter tried to make the succession to the throne dependent on the reigning monarch's choice. As a matter of fact, there was no clear, unambiguous system of succession. The oldest son succeeded as a matter of custom, but in the absence (or incapacity) of such an heir, tradi-

Peter I—Engravings from wax masks, 1719

tion was not a sure guide, as was demonstrated at the death of Tsar Feodor. In any event, following the flight, return, arrest, and death of his only son, Tsarevich Alexis,[2] Peter decreed that thereafter every sovereign would be free to appoint as successor whomever he pleased. Peter himself, however, did not have a chance to exercise this option, for in January 1725, he died after a sudden, short illness, without naming a successor. Peter's legislation, and the accidental high incidence of women on the throne in the eighteenth century, resulted in numerous succession crises. Each one was resolved by a palace coup carried out with the help of the military, with foreign intrigues and monies contributing to determine the outcome.

---

[2] Peter's son by his first wife, Tsarevich Alexis, proved a great disappointment to his father. He did not acquire the knowledge and skills Peter insisted he must have and was, apparently, quite unsympathetic to his father's policies. Alexis was surrounded by a great many people who were attached to his mother's court and he also was used to intercede with his father on behalf of various traditionalists who had fallen out of favor. Eventually, after the death of his young German wife in childbirth, Alexis fled to Austria and from there to Naples. A. Tolstoy managed to find out his hideout and beguiled him to return to Russia. Alexis was arrested and brought to trial on charges of treason and conspiracy against his father. He died while in prison, probably as a result of the tortures to which he was subjected during his interrogation.

Prince Alexander Menshikov, Peter's favorite

Succession

At the death of Peter I, there were four contenders for the succession: his grandson Peter, son of Tsarevich Alexis, still a child and for whom a regency would be required; his oldest daughter, Anne, married to the Duke of Holstein; his younger daughter, Elizabeth; and his widow, Catherine, his second wife, whom he had crowned empress not long before. There was some question about the canonic validity of Peter's marriage to Catherine, and consequently the legitimacy of their daughters' birth (they were born before the marriage had received the sanction of the Church, a sanction that was, moreover, of doubtful canonicity, since Peter's first wife was still alive). The boy Peter had been brought up in his father's and paternal grand-

mother's circle. It was therefore assumed that his accession would
bring to power the party of traditionalists—more particularly, those
who craved revenge for their long humiliation and the death of
Tsarevich Alexis. Anne's accession would mean the preponderant
influence of the Duke of Holstein and his German advisors, who in
the opinion of Peter's dignitaries already had too much power.
Elizabeth was too young, and it would have been embarrassing to
give preference to her over her older sister.

The choice of the most powerful dignitaries fell on Catherine,
Peter's widow, a simple servant girl from the Baltic provinces who
had been the mistress of her captor, Field Marshal Sheremetev, and
then of Prince A. D. Menshikov, before becoming concubine and
finally legal spouse of the Emperor. In the final analysis, Catherine
did not win out, as is usually claimed, because of the court's and
the Guards' fear of the entourage of the boy Peter and of a return
to Muscovite ways. The boy was still very young (he was born in
October 1715) and could not have had any will of his own, and
his entourage could have been pushed aside by those in control. The
decisive factor in proclaiming Catherine I Empress was Prince Menshikov's personal interests. Menshikov had risen from a lowly status
to the position of friend and most powerful dignitary of Peter I; at
the moment of the Emperor's death, he was virtually "assistant tsar"
(in spite of an earlier temporary loss of Peter's confidence and the
justified accusations of corruption and abuse that had been leveled
at him). It would be easy for him to preserve his powerful position
under Catherine, who had been his mistress, who knew him as her
husband's loyal collaborator and friend, and to whom she could
safely entrust state affairs for which she had neither much interest
nor understanding (she was barely literate).

Menshikov, assisted by Count A. Tolstoy and other dignitaries,
brought the Guards regiments to the palace and had them shout for
Catherine, who rewarded them with gifts, drink, and a smile. This
set a precedent that was to be followed many times in the course
of the eighteenth century. It may be argued that in 1725 the Guards
acted in defense of their group interests, which might have been
threatened by a return to power of the traditionalist boiars, nobles,
and clergy; but such a consideration lost its raison d'être in subsequent years. In later coups, the Guards participated in support of
this or that ruler or court faction merely in the expectation of earning special rewards and gifts as *individuals,* or because they wanted
to get rid of a group of favorites or dignitaries who had not been
very generous to them. As a matter of fact, the Guards ceased to
play an active role in palace coups after their composition had

become socially homogeneous—after their regiments turned into the exclusive preserve of an "aristocratic" elite.

Because Catherine neglected government affairs, absolute power was in fact exercised by Menshikov, who used the position to fill his own pockets and get even with his enemies. But a favorite who depends on a passive and ignorant ruler like Catherine I cannot long remain in power unless he is also supported by others of the ruling clique. Within less than a year, Menshikov was compelled to share his power with other "fledglings of Peter's nest." The most important officials forced the creation of a Supreme Privy Council (*Verkhovnyi tainyi sovet*), of which Menshikov was still a member, and a most influential one. The Supreme Privy Council became in fact the ruler of Russia, relegating the Senate and the Holy Synod to subordinate positions. Contrary to the belief held by some historians, the council did not attempt to undo Peter's reforms. Constituted by Peter's former high officials, the Supreme Privy Council continued his policy, although emphasizing more the country's economic recuperation and allowing society to digest the cultural and institutional innovations and territorial acquisitions. Members of the Supreme Privy Council set their sights lower, relaxed the pressure, and used blandishments in preference to the threats with which Peter had been so lavish. The council did remarkably well, all things considered, in keeping the Petrine machine going and in preserving the first emperor's diplomatic and cultural gains. By keeping the empire at peace, the army personnel could be reduced by granting extended leaves of absence to the officers; the peasantry was encouraged to do its share and pay taxes in full by canceling arrears and delegating the collection of dues to local officials.

In 1727 Catherine I died. Secure in its position as the principal governing body, the Supreme Privy Council decided to put Peter II, the grandson of Peter the Great, on the throne. Menshikov concurred, as he had hopes of gaining control of the boy emperor by having him marry his own daughter Maria. But for once Menshikov had overreached himself. The other members of the Supreme Privy Council—especially the Dolgorukys—toppled him; Peter's erstwhile closest associate was arrested, deprived of all his ranks, his vast fortune confiscated, and he himself exiled to Berezovo in Siberia, where he died a few years later. The Supreme Privy Council was reorganized to accommodate several new members of the families of Princes Dolgoruky and Golitsyn, although its policies did not change materially. The Dolgoruky family hoped to gain control over Peter II through the influence exercised by his equerry, Prince Ivan Dolgoruky. Like Menshikov before them, they hoped to become

Field Marshall V. V. Dolgoruky

virtual masters of the empire by marrying Princess Catherine Dolgoruky, Ivan's sister, to the emperor. Their calculations were upset,
however, by Peter II's catching smallpox and dying after a few days
of illness in January 1730. The throne was vacant again.

The most intelligent and sophisticated member of the Supreme
Privy Council, Prince D. M. Golitsyn, who had had a distinguished
career under Peter I as governor of Kiev and head of the Treasury
College, and who had been a member of the Supreme Privy Council
since its inception, decided that the time had come, as he expressed
it, "to make things easier for ourselves." He suggested that Anna,
Peter the Great's niece (daughter of his half-brother and co-tsar,
Ivan V) and dowager duchess of Courland, be proclaimed empress,
but with the proviso that she would agree to a number of conditions
(eight in all) which secured the primacy of the Supreme Privy
Council. His colleagues agreed, and Prince Luke Dolgoruky was
dispatched to Mittau, Anna's residence in Courland, to offer her the
crown. Happy to escape from an obscure provincial life, she accepted
without hesitation; most likely, too, she was advised by the former
Procurator-General of the Senate, P. Iaguzhinsky, that the situation
in Moscow was fluid and gave her room for action. Indeed, as Anna

Prince V. L. Dolgoruky

was slowly making her way to Moscow, rumors spread that the Supreme Privy Council was trying to consolidate its position and introduce government by oligarchy. This alarmed the high-ranking officers and officials, the so-called *generalitet* (that is, those who held a rank equal to that of general in the Table of Ranks), who were afraid they would be excluded from power by the oligarchs of the Supreme Privy Council. The reaction of the *generalitet* reflected the perennial Russian fear of rule by aristocrats or favorites which, it seemed, always led to internal dissension and to foreign ingerence (the example of Poland was a constant warning). The rank-and-file nobles, too, wanted a share in the benefits of power and influence on their own merits, without having to become—as had been the case in the seventeenth century—the retainers or clients of a few great families.

Forced by the agitation of the *generalitet* to make concessions, Prince Golitsyn tried to placate them by inviting them to offer their own suggestions and plans. But as the *generalitet* started to meet and work out their various proposals, the rank-and-file service noblemen, who had flocked to Moscow in large numbers for the expected coronation and wedding of Peter II, could not be prevented from also engaging in meetings and agitation. In simplest terms, Golitsyn's conditions for Anna restricted her autocratic power by requiring her to seek the advice and consent of the Supreme Privy Council in decisions affecting war, peace, her own succession, and promotions to higher ranks. The *generalitet* suggested that the sovereign also seek the advice and consent of an enlarged Senate of up to a hundred members, drawn from the upper echelons of the service hierarchy; and that the Supreme Privy Council be either abolished or its membership enlarged, with no one family having more than one member in it. The rank-and-file noblemen simply demanded the restoration to Anna of her ancestors' full autocratic prerogatives and the abolition of the Supreme Privy Council. Indeed, they felt they had a better chance to obtain rewards and promotions from the discretionary authority of a monarch than from any oligarchic body on which they would have no representation. Both *generalitet* and rank-and-file also requested that a special school be set up for children of the nobility, so that they need not go through the ranks to become officers; that leaves from service be given more liberally; that the compulsory lifelong service obligation be limited to twenty-five or thirty years; and finally, that the law of single inheritance be abrogated.

Upon her arrival in Moscow, Anna was informed of the opposition to the plans of the Supreme Privy Council. She contrived to call a general meeting of the nobility, at which she asked them whether they approved of the conditions she had signed in Mittau. The crowd shouted its disapproval, and thereupon "She deigned to tear them up" in the presence of the helpless Supreme Privy Council. Anna then "graciously accepted" the petition drawn up by the rank-and-file nobles asking her to resume her full autocratic power and rule with "maternal benevolence." In due course, the empress established a Corps of Cadets (1731) and abolished the law of single inheritance (1734), but the nobility had to wait for the reign of Elizabeth for an effective easing of the compulsory service obligation.

Restored to her unlimited autocratic power, Anna ruled with anything but benevolence. She gave free rein to her German favorites, Ernst Biron (Bühren) who was made Duke of Courland, and R. Löwenwolde, whom she had brought from Mittau. These men took advantage of their position to acquire large fortunes through graft and corruption; buttressed by Anna's confidence, they met any challenge to their influence with brutal ferocity. The population groaned under an increasingly heavy burden of taxation, while the upper classes were kept in mortal fear of denunciations to the police that knew no distinction of rank, wealth, or merit. But the *Biro-novshchina,* as this brutal domination of the German favorites was

called, was more than just negative.[Biron himself was not without
ability, although his lust for power and his greed prevented him
from being a statesman. A successful war against Turkey secured
Azov again for Russia; the first steps were taken to colonize the
Ukraine; an aggressive policy was pursued in promoting Russian
expansion and peasant settlement in the East. Peter's administrative
changes were retained, and the operation of the new institutions
gradually became smoother and more efficient. Instead of the
Supreme Privy Council, Anna established a Cabinet of Ministers
to provide continuity and direction for policy planning, while main-
taining the Senate in a subordinate position. The cabinet's *spiritus
rector* became the highly capable (albeit unsavory) Artemii Volynsky.
Volynsky promoted trade with the East and had plans for a dramatic
expansion of Russia's economic and industrial potential. The plans
went unrealized, for he fell victim to Biron's displeasure (not without
cause, since he was probably plotting to overthrow the favorite). He
was tried for treason and executed in 1740.]

Anna died childless in 1740 after naming her infant great-nephew
Ivan (Antonovich) to succeed her under the regency of his mother,
Anna Leopol'dovna, who was married to the Duke of Brunswick.
At first the regent-mother remained under the virtual control of
Biron, but his arrogant despotism led her to support Field Marshal
B. Münnich in overthrowing and exiling the hated duke of Courland.
As far as the Russians were concerned, Münnich's coup only perpet-
uated the rule by Germans, albeit of more intelligent and conscien-
tious ones. The real head of the civil administration was the veteran
Count A. Osterman, a Westphalian who had begun his career as a
translator in the College for Foreign Affairs under Peter the Great
and had then become a member of the Supreme Privy Council and
Cabinet of Ministers. Angry at being excluded from the imperial
bounty by the Germans, the Russian nobility—especially the officers
and soldiers of the Guards—looked for another ruler who would
favor them. Their eyes fell on Elizabeth, the daughter of Peter the
Great; a friendly, gay, attractive person, she was popular among
the Guards and the Russian members of the court. Her various
amorous affairs also brought her into close contact with some of the
foreign diplomats, particularly the French Minister, Marquis de La
Chétardie, who hoped to bring about a Franco-Russian alliance
against Austria and Prussia. La Chétardie was generous with his
government's money, so that in addition to her personal charms,
Elizabeth also had something substantial to offer her supporters. On
the night of November 24–25, 1741, at the head of the Preobrazhensky Guards regiment, Elizabeth arrested her cousin the regent,
proclaimed herself empress, and sent the infant Ivan VI, with his

parents, Marshal Münnich, Count Osterman, and their hangers-on into exile.

For twenty years the Russian Empire was ruled by the gay, lazy, pleasure-loving, spendthrift daughter of Peter the Great. It was an important, and in many ways seminal, period for Russia's development; unfortunately, it has been poorly studied thus far. Russian cultural life had a remarkable flowering, mainly at the court and in the two capitals. The reign was also significant from the point of view of Russian diplomacy and imperial policy. It was marked by the consolidation of the colonization of the Ukraine and of the southeastern frontier, and by the final elimination of Sweden as a serious threat. At the end of her reign, Elizabeth also witnessed Russia's first great triumph in Central Europe, when her troops defeated King Frederick II and occupied Berlin. It was clear proof that the Russian military establishment, whose organization and training had not been allowed to lapse since the death of Peter the Great, was at least equal, if not outright superior, to the best army of Europe at the time. But equally important were the new orientation in economic policy and the gradual emergence of political patterns that were to dominate Russian public life well into the nineteenth century. Unfortunately, the details of these developments have not yet been fully elucidated, and we must content ourselves with a few general observations.

Elizabeth was not hard-working, energetic, or absorbed in politics; she wanted to enjoy herself in full freedom and security. Like every female ruler without official husband, she had many personal favorites, among whom the best known was Alexis Razumovsky (probably her morganatic husband). But the dominant influence was exercised by Chancellor A. P. Bestuzhev-Riumin in foreign affairs and the brothers Peter and Alexander Shuvalov in domestic policy. During her long reign, therefore, a stable pattern of administrative organization and political authority could develop, since the management of the empire was left to these advisors and to high state officials. Having ascended the throne on the promise of a return to her father's system, Elizabeth abolished the Cabinet of Ministers and restored the Senate to the position of principal government institution— although at the time of the Seven Years' War, she instituted a Special Conference at the Imperial Court that functioned not only as a policy planning and coordinating body, but also as an organ of government in matters directly related to the conduct of the war (supplies, transportation, recruitment and training, diplomatic negotiations). The Senate in her reign supervised the colleges and exercised the overall direction of policy on a day-to-day basis, including direct correspondence with and supervision of provincial governors and institutions.

The Senate's leading role had not come about suddenly by concerted design; rather, it had evolved gradually over a period of years as practices were systematized and the corps of officials acquired some stability and homogeneity. Indeed, it is in this latter respect particularly that the long and relatively undisturbed reign of Elizabeth proved so seminal. What happened was the gradual emergence of an identifiable group of individuals (and families) who formed a permanent body of high officials and dignitaries occupying the key positions in the state. They were the heads of important Colleges and members of the Senate and of the Special Conference. They controlled and directed the subordinate staff of professionals from among whom they on occasion coopted new members (D. V. Volkov, Secretary of the Conference, for example). Quite a few of the select group came from old service families, but not always from the most prominent and wealthiest; others came from the rank-and-file nobility, but established firm ties with the better families through marriage.[3] This group of individuals and families consolidated their position in the principal institutions of government and at court in order to acquire wealth, influence, and command of the main levers of power, and to transmit these to their children or relatives and clients. Such were, for instance, Golitsyn, Trubetskoy, Shuvalov, Vorontsov, Glebov, Repnin, Panin, Shakhovskoy, from among the old families, and the relative newcomers to distinction, "professionals" like I. I. Nepliuev and Volkov. In retrospect, we can see that they endeavored to secure for the chief government institutions, in particular for the Senate, continuity of membership and authority that would routinize their political and administrative roles and permit them to enjoy a large degree of autonomy of action in ordinary affairs, letting the autocrat exercise her sovereign power of ultimate decision and intervention only in extraordinary cases. Carried to its logical conclusion, this pattern would have provided a firm foundation for a *Rechtsstaat* controlled by an aristocracy of office. Paradoxically, such a development would have meant fulfilling the program of Prince Golitsyn in 1730, only on a broader base and in more bureaucratic form, as it was perhaps envisaged by the *generalitet.*

---

[3] In a sense, it was also a continuation of the system of clients (personal and family) that had been so important in Muscovy in the seventeenth century. Incidentally, the notion and practice of "clientèle" were also major elements in the formation of the "ruling class" in Ancien Régime France and in England in the eighteenth century. The latter situation may also help to explain the great appeal England had for Russian dignitaries as a model to be emulated (the Vorontsovs, for example, were notorious Anglomaniacs).

Of particular interest is the striking fact that the ruling group under Elizabeth displayed much greater sensitivity to the empire's economic development, from which they hoped also to benefit personally. Indeed, with a few exceptions, the nobility had not taken Peter the Great's invitation to become actively involved in economic entrepreneurship. Because of their poverty and the obligation of lifelong, permanent service, the rank-and-file nobles could not— even if they had wished to—be efficient agricultural producers and entrepreneurs. The economic aspects of national life had not been completely ignored by the Russian government since Peter I, but those in power had looked at them from the point of view of immediate fiscal needs or as a means for rapid personal enrichment at the expense of the state. This was no longer the case with men like the brothers Shuvalov, Prince Ia. P. Shakhovskoy, the Vorontsov brothers, Volkov. They too had selfish motives, as we shall see, but they realized the necessity for a long-range, comprehensive approach to stimulating the economic expansion of the empire, an approach in which the government would have to play an important role. At the same time, they felt that economic development would be most ·efficiently furthered by private enterprises given state assistance.

As formulated and implemented by Count Peter Shuvalov, the economic policy of Elizabeth's reign presented a double aspect: The first, which in the long run proved the least successful, consisted in attracting individual entrepreneurs (preference being given to the Shuvalovs and their clients) by leasing or selling them state manufactures and mines, or by granting them monopoly privileges. Only the wealthiest and best-connected courtiers could take advantage of this policy; they, however, rarely had the skill, perseverance, or commitment to be successful entrepreneurs. The state was often forced to buy back the enterprises at a loss—and the operation turned out to have been a thinly disguised form of graft or bounty given to select favorites. In a few instances, the noble entrepreneurs were bought out by merchants, who were slowly beginning to play a significant role in the industrial development of the country (for example, in the Urals). The second aspect of Elizabeth's economic policy, and the one which proved to be of significant and lasting impact, consisted in freeing domestic trade from the burdens of internal tariffs and tolls. In the course of her reign all domestic tariffs were abolished, so that local commerce at long last could move freely. Her successor, Peter III, only put the finishing touch to the policy by eliminating the remaining urban tolls on local peasant trade. But transportation costs and difficulties remained great.

After what has just been said about the governing elite and its economic orientation, it is not surprising to learn that legislation under Elizabeth favored the nobility, both in social and economic terms. One series of measures aimed at limiting the access of non-nobles, primarily the sons of priests and soldiers, to higher positions in the military and civil services. While the provisions of the Table of Ranks were not invalidated, their application became very restrictive. At the same time, the first significant steps were taken to limit the duration of the nobility's compulsory state service, first to thirty, then to twenty-five and even twenty years. This policy also aimed at encouraging noble landowners to turn their attention and energies to the management of their estates. To this end, measures were taken to confirm and reinforce the nobleman's authority over his serfs. The noble landowner received full police powers over his peasants, including the right to resettle them in Siberia (1760, with full recruit credit), and to exile them at hard labor (1765); then the peasants were forbidden to address complaints to the sovereign against their owners (1767).[4] We have already noted that noble entrepreneurs were freely granted state subsidies and monopoly rights. Elizabeth was also particularly generous in giving away state lands (with peasants) to courtiers, favorites, dignitaries, and generals. Naturally, noblemen received favored treatment in the allocation of free lands and rights to settle peasants in the Ukraine. Largely under the influence of her favorite, Razumovsky, Elizabeth granted to the native Ukrainian Cossack nobles equality of status with the Russian nobility, thereby extending their rights over peasants.

Elizabeth died on Christmas Day, 1761, and was succeeded by her nephew, Peter III, whom she had "imported" from Holstein and attempted to groom for the Russian throne. In this she was quite unsuccessful, for Peter remained at an arrested stage of emotional and intellectual development, never took to things Russian, was dominated by an exclusive concern for parades and uniforms, and had a childish admiration for Frederick II and for Prussia. Upon acceding to the throne, he immediately stopped military operations against Frederick II and signed a treaty by which he gave up all Russian advantages, and in addition pledged to support Prussia in the future. This policy, along with Peter's obvious scorn for the Russian Church and language, aroused a sense of national shame and outrage among members of the army. Peter's personal conduct did not endear him to St. Petersburg society either; he was boorish, got drunk every evening with a few German cronies, and behaved in an insulting manner toward his wife, Catherine. Cleverly manipulated

---

[4] Though the final versions of these acts were issued only in the first years of the reign of Catherine II, they had been prepared under Elizabeth.

Catherine II—engraving by Radig, 1768

by Catherine and fearful of being sent to fight in Denmark for Peter's interests and possessions in Holstein, the Guards regiments helped to overthrow the emperor after a reign of only six months. Catherine was proclaimed empress; first imprisoned, Peter was probably murdered by his guards. Despite its brevity, the reign of Peter III is notable for several measures that had lasting repercussions on the social and economic development of Russia; these will be discussed in their proper context in later chapters.

The very long rule of Catherine II, 1762–1796, was one of the most seminal periods for the formation of modern Russia's culture and polity. Unfortunately, it has not yet found a historian worthy of it. One of the factors that contributed to make the reign such an important one was no doubt the empress herself. Born in 1729 into a petty German princely family (Anhalt-Zerbst), she was married at fifteen to the boorish, perhaps retarded, and in all respects unsuitable Peter. But from the moment she set foot in Russia, she was determined to become its ruler. She spent the long lonely years when she was merely the wife of the heir presumptive educating herself, developing a superb political and diplomatic talent. When she became sole mistress of the empire at the age of thirty-three, she was ready: she had a general idea of where she wanted to lead the country, and she possessed the psychological insight and political tact necessary to command men. Like any skilled politician, she knew when to change tactics, adjust her goals to circumstances, and shift direction. In addition, her own intellectual vanity and her demagoguery led her to adopt prevailing ideas and attitudes thus giving a particularly appealing form to her deeds. In spite of her tactical flexibility and her basic commitment to the sociopolitical status quo, one can discern a continuity in long-range aims and general approach, both of which she clearly formulated long before she had acquired the power to put them into practice.

Largely under the influence of her wide reading of the German *Kameralisten*, natural law jurists, and French *philosophes*, Catherine's basic political program consisted in maximizing the economic potential of her empire so as to increase the wealth of the state, enhance the power of the government, and promote the welfare of the people. With respect to the last aim, she naturally thought first of furthering the prosperity of the ruling elite, and second that of the energetic and successful urban classes; only last did she concern herself with the individual serf and peasant. In other words, the goal of her government was a better and more active exploitation of all the physical resources and human potential of the empire. If successful, she would also possess the means to pursue an ambitious and effective imperial policy. As a good student of eighteenth-century thought, however, Catherine II also believed that her aims would be best served if her subjects were encouraged to pursue their own self-interest. To this end, her policy was to foster individual enterprise, activity, and direct participation in the economic and cultural life of the nation. The function of the state was to provide the necessary security and protection to property and person, to stimulate and assist, but not to undertake and control everything.

Catherine aimed at fostering individual and collective action and anchoring it securely in the circumscribed sphere of private economic and social concerns, but clearly excluding it from participation in all and any political matters. The legislation that Catherine planned, and most of the measures she undertook in internal affairs, were to serve this ultimate purpose, at least until the French Revolution threw her into a panic. Had it succeeded, the policy would have brought the society, economy, culture, and political organization of the Russian Empire to a level equal with that of the more advanced and prosperous German states—the enlightened absolute monarchies based on estates (*Ständestaat*)—for example Prussia, Austria, Württemberg. Seen from this perspective, Catherine II was truly an enlightened despot, like Frederick II of Prussia and Emperor Joseph II, although she had to operate within a more primitive social framework. She was actually realizing the ultimate intention of Peter the Great, who had hoped for a Russian society composed of economically and culturally active and enterprising individuals and groups. But whereas Peter I relied exclusively on government direction, guidance, and control at every step, Catherine hoped to foster and rely on the initiative of her subjects.

It is in this light, too, it seems to me, that we should view Catherine's well-known convocation of a Legislative Commission (1767) and her much-publicized Nakaz (Instruction) for its deputies. Her motives in convoking deputies to draft a code of laws have not been fully elucidated by historians, nor may they ever be capable of elucidation. An important consideration, and one that has been persuasively argued by Sacke,[5] was no doubt the desire to obtain the sanction of a broad sector of "public opinion" for her own usurpation of the throne. Catherine's desire to "show off"—for the same purpose—to fellow rulers and opinion makers in Western Europe also played a role in the decision. And there was the simple good reason that Russia needed a new code of laws, although success in such a difficult and technical enterprise could hardly be expected from a large assembly of elected deputies. Liberal historiography to the contrary notwithstanding, one thing seems quite evident: Catherine did not intend or expect the deputies to draft a constitution; nor was her own Nakaz a blueprint for anything even remotely resembling a political settlement. Rather, it would seem from the text of the Nakaz and the organization of the commission's debates that Catherine merely intended a formal acceptance by Russian "public opinion" of the basic concepts underlying her program.[6] The Nakaz offers primarily a blueprint of the rules needed to secure personal safety, property, and freedom of action in the economic and cultural domains of the free subjects of the empire (that is, excluding the serfs).[7] This explains why in the Nakaz so much attention was devoted to judicial procedures and to the law of property. It may be an exaggeration to say that the Nakaz provided the foundation and framework for the development of a genuinely modern civil society

---

[5] G. Sacke, *Die Gesetzgebende Kommission Katharinas II. Ein Beitrag zur Geschichte des Absolutismus in Russland.* Breslau, 1940.

[6] Priority was given to discussion, in committees, of draft proposals for the organization of estates of the population. The discussions and debates in the general assembly of the commission were strictly controlled by Catherine II through the marshal (president) of the commission, General I. I. Bibikov, whom she had carefully chosen for the task.

[7] Although Catherine had originally intended to include serfs in the *pays légal* that was to emerge from the commission's work.

(bürgerliche Gesellschaft); but had it been implemented, it would no doubt have been a first step in that direction, for it would have provided one necessary condition—namely, the rule of law with respect to the protection of person and property.

The Commission did not fulfill Catherine's expectations, and it was not allowed to complete its work. Yet it did accomplish one thing: it gave Catherine—and future historians—much valuable information on the conditions, needs, and desires of many of her subjects. It was information she took into account in her subsequent legislation, even if she did not by any means act positively on the wishes and requests expressed by the deputies. The calling of the Commission had quite obviously a great impact on public opinion, such as it was in Russia at the time. It probably raised many a false hope (or fear) of a fundamental restructuring of the Russian polity, and such erroneous expectations played no mean role in creating the ferment that led to the Pugachev rebellion. Of even greater significance was the fact that Catherine's Nakaz, as well as the elections and debates of the deputies, did familiarize the educated segment of Russian society with the basic concepts of a modern and open approach to economic progress, law, and social welfare. The subsequent inclusion of the Nakaz in the Complete Collection of Russian Laws (Polnoe sobranie zakonov rossiiskoi imperii, 1830) clearly shows that the progress-minded bureaucrats of the first half of the nineteenth century believed that its basic principles set guidelines for later legislation. Last, but not least, many contemporary and subsequent critics of Russia's social and political system turned to the Nakaz to substantiate and justify their reform proposals.[8]

The policy of freeing the energies of the individual subject and of providing a corporate framework for his security found its legislative and administrative implementation with the reorganization of local government in 1775 and the establishment of corporate estates by the charters to the nobility and to the towns (1785). All these acts will be discussed at their proper place in the topical chapters.

Catherine's diplomacy, like that of all European rulers in the eighteenth century, was motivated in the first place by considerations of power politics and the changing constellation of alliances and alignments. Yet her foreign policy, to some extent, also reflected and illustrated the overall aims of government we have noted. She earned the admiration of her contemporaries, and in some cases their gratitude, by her impressive successes in diplomacy and war. Indeed, her reign was marked by the greatest territorial acquisitions since the

---

[8] We find evidence for it among the writings of I. Pnin and V. Popugaev in the 1800s and in those of N. Turgenev and of the secret societies after 1815.

The Bronze Horseman—Catherine the Great's monument to Peter the Great

conquests of Kazan, Astrakhan, and Siberia in the sixteenth century. Two successful wars against Turkey (1768–1774, ending in the Treaty of Kuchuk-Kainardji, and 1787–1792, leading to the Treaty of Jassy) fulfilled Peter the Great's old ambitions by consecrating Russian possession of the northern shores of the Black Sea and of the Crimea, and laid the groundwork for further penetration into the Caucasus. The Treaty of Kuchuk-Kainardji also gave Russia freedom of navigation on the Black Sea and the role of protector of the Sultan's Christian subjects, a clause that subsequently was to offer convenient pretexts for intervention. The centuries-old threat of Turkish and Crimean Tartar incursions into Central Russia and the Ukraine had come to an end. This major success permitted the consolidation of Russian control over the Kirghiz and Bashkir steppes north and east of the Caspian Sea.

The best-known, as well as the most notorious, achievement of

Catherine's foreign policy was her participation in the partitions of Poland. By the terms of the partitions, Russia not only received the territories of the former Grand Duchy of Lithuania, which Moscow's rulers had claimed as their patrimony since the fifteenth century, but also parts of the kingdom of Poland. Diplomatically, the partitions forced Russia into a lasting alliance with Prussia.

But as important as the acquisition of new territories was their economic and social integration into the Russian polity. It is here that the empress' domestic and foreign policy goals were intertwined: much empty and undeveloped territory was given the institutional means of becoming an important productive element in the total economy of the empire. Such was the case of the policies aimed at the incorporation and colonization of New Russia (*Novorossiiskaia guberniia*)—the southern and southeastern lands between Central Russia, the Black and the Caspian Seas; the foundation and development of new ports and cities, and the beginnings of exports through the Black Sea.

Finally, it should be noted, the reign of Catherine II was one of the most fecund periods in the development of Russian culture and literature. While still dependent on the cultural and spiritual resources of the West, as illustrated by the architectural triumphs in and around St. Petersburg, the brilliant court life, and Catherine's own contacts with the intellectual luminaries of France, the educated elite of Russia was beginning to display a creative originality that proved to be the foundation of a truly national and modern culture and literature in the next century. The intellectual ferment, however, coupled with the economic and political developments of Catherine's reign, brought about the first manifestations of a critical spirit with respect to the social system and the practices of the government. There emerged a new outlook on the downtrodden peasant masses, an outlook that was to be the harbinger of a new social and cultural force: the intelligentsia. Coinciding with the beginning of the French Revolution, these intellectual stirrings were harshly repressed by the empress, who ended her reign on a note of tyranny. Her death thus seemed a welcome relief, although in retrospect her reign appeared as one of the most brilliant and creative periods of imperial Russia.

Catherine's son, Paul, born in 1754, ascended the throne after a very long wait. He had been kept from participation in the affairs of state by his mother, ever jealous of her power, and he was embittered and eager to make up for lost time. Once in power, he proceeded to undo much of his mother's legislation. Yet, Paul was not completely unprepared for his role as tsar; his tutor, Count N. I. Panin, had instilled in him the more progressive views of the "aristocratic" party. On the basis of Paul's notes for a will and the draft of a proclamation (or oath) of accession, it has been argued that Paul seriously intended to introduce a genuine *bürgerliche Gesellschaft* into Russia. He insisted that the nobility take their duty to serve seriously; he tried to limit the exploitation of serf labor by landowners by restricting the lord's corvée to three days a week. The decree did not remain a dead letter altogether, for—as Soviet historians have recently shown—we have evidence of several instances of prosecutions in connection with violations of this decree. Paul also seems to have had plans for a reorganization of the administration, and a wider role for the Senate. In fact, he did succeed in further transforming the cumbersome colleges into monocratic departments. Finally, he extricated Russia from a war by coming to terms with the First Consul, Napoleon Bonaparte.

Whatever his good intentions, Paul's reign was marred by his capricious character and the unpredictable, arbitrary nature of his behavior. Isolated from society, the court, and the government by his suspicious mother, separated from his erstwhile tutors and his friends who could have exercised a beneficent influence, Paul grew to be unduly jealous and touchy about his authority. As long as his mother's reign lasted, he lived in honorable exile in the palace of Gatchina, near St. Petersburg, where he freely indulged in his favorite pastime: training, drilling, and parading his small garrison. Enamored of Prussian militarism like his father, he scorned the flighty and luxury-loving courtiers and commanders of Catherine II, even the military genius Field Marshal A. V. Suvorov. "Paradomania," as Prince A. Czartoryski called it, became Paul's passion, and the emperor subordinated everything to neat and diligent performance on the parade ground.

When he ascended the throne, he installed his cronies from Gatchina (for example, Baron A. Arakcheev) in the Winter Palace and proceeded to "tighten up" St. Petersburg society on the model of his garrison. He tried to impose his Spartan military outlook on the capital by means of strict discipline, police control, and harsh censorship. He banned everything that was even remotely connected with the free ways of the West, in particular everything that could be reminiscent of the French Revolution. (He went to such ludicrous extremes as forbidding the use of some words, the wearing of round hats, the importation of sheet music and books of mathematics.) Having accepted the Grand Mastery of the Order of St. John of Jerusalem (the Maltese Order), his foreign policy became determined by the needs and interests of the order as well as by those of Russia (for example, the sending of Cossacks to conquer India). His ways and orders were a nightmare for the officers of the Guards and St.

Petersburg society; his unpredictable and violent fits of rage were a threat to the security and freedom of all those who had to deal with him. It is true, he could be made to realize and right his mistakes, and he was not devoid of magnanimity, but these qualities did not make up for the harm resulting from his outbreaks. With respect to the administration, his capricious temper resulted in a constant turnover of ministers and advisors. For instance, in his short reign the office of procurator-general of the Senate alone was held by six persons in succession. Not surprisingly, therefore, the plot to eliminate him was hatched within his own entourage. Led by the emperor's "favorite," Count von der Pahlen, military governor of St. Petersburg, assisted by General Bennigsen and Vice-Chancellor Panin, the conspirators murdered the emperor on the night of March 11, 1801.

The short reign of Paul I was experienced as a nightmare by Russia's educated society in the two capitals, although the common people seemed to have had genuine affection for him, and he even appears not to have been unpopular with the provincial nobility despite his efforts at putting them back into service and at limiting their rights over the labor of serfs. But the sophisticated society of St. Petersburg, accustomed to the intellectual playfulness and excitement of Catherine's court (notwithstanding the repression in her last years), could not accept Paul's style. The members of this elite would not submit to the capricious and brutal outbursts of the sovereign and his humiliating treatment of his officers and courtiers. By the end of the eighteenth century, the Russian nobleman of the capital had become too strongly imbued with a sense of his own worth and dignity to allow himself to be treated like a servant (kholop). For this reason, Paul's death was greeted with jubilation by the inhabitants of St. Petersburg. The general feeling was that such tyranny should not be permitted to happen again. His successor, Alexander I (1801–1825), was therefore greeted with enthusiasm, and the most optimistic expectations for political reform seemed justified when the young emperor proclaimed his intention to reign in the spirit of his grandmother, Catherine II.

In an autocracy, the personality of the ruler is a historical factor that cannot be ignored. Contemporaries, as well as later historians, have always had great difficulty in defining and assessing the character of Alexander I. It is not an accident that he was called "beguiler" ("charmeur"), "Greek of the Lower Empire," "Crowned Hamlet," "blessed." Alexander apparently had the gift of appearing to his interlocutor as the latter wished to see him, although he still acted as he had decided to in the first place—hence the impression of wavering and duplicity he created. He was an excellent diplomat

and most enjoyed this aspect of government, refusing to delegate it to anyone. He may have developed this gift of appearing to please everyone because of the early necessity in which he found himself of having to show affection to both his grandmother and his father. Be that as it may, his youthfulness and charm, both of which he retained until his death, served to create for him a reputation of benevolence.

We have mentioned how society reacted to his accession. Any discussion, consideration or implementation of even the most modest reform was not only well received, but was interpreted in a much more liberal sense than was justified either by the government's actual deeds or its intentions. This misunderstanding explains the disappointment experienced by the members of the progressive elite and the resulting opposition to Alexander in the last decade of his reign.[9]

Before proceeding with a brief account of the reign, a few words may be in order at this point about the changes in the character of Russian educated society that become noticeable in the first quarter of the nineteenth century. Coinciding with the beginning of the new century, a new and different generation of educated Russians made its appearance. In contrast to the intellectual elite of Catherine's time, the young men who achieved maturity in the years of "Alexander's golden beginnings" combined the moral concepts of the *Aufklärung* and of the French *philosophes* with the emotional passion and enthusiasm of sentimentalism and early Romanticism. It was the generation of *Sturm und Drang,* but it was much more involved in the rationalism and social concerns of the eighteenth-century Enlightenment. Most significant of all, the young generation looked with very different eyes at the Russian serf: to them, the serfs were human beings, with pure souls and genuine human needs; and it behooved the elite to help them attain a higher level of culture and well-being. Unlike their elders, the young elite approached social and political issues openly and rationally, basing their arguments and ideals on Catherine's notions of humanitarianism, benevolence, reliance on individual activity protected by law. In a sense, they were literally children of the Nakaz, but their commitment was laden with a passion, an emotional involvement that would hardly have pleased its imperial author. They burned with a desire to help the emperor and his government fulfill the highest ideals and humanitarian goals

---

[9] Liberal historiography, which dominated the field in the nineteenth and early twentieth centuries, incorporated this attitude. It explains the notion of the two distinct periods of Alexander's reign—the first, constitutional and liberal; the second, reactionary—that is still to be found in most textbooks.

of the Enlightenment. They generated an optimistic mood of impending reform; they expected to be drawn into social and political work. They felt confirmed in their expectations by the government's lenient policy on censorship and its encouragement of new publications and serious discussion of economic and social problems.

The reaction of public opinion to Paul's reign and the mood of the younger generation combined to create an atmosphere of exhilaration and expectation. Alexander I eagerly responded to it, the more so since the constellation of forces at court compelled him to take energetic action to consolidate his rule. The young monarch and his advisors cleverly took advantage of the pressure of society to bring about a series of much needed and significant reforms in the administrative structure of the empire. We shall examine these reforms, along with their political and social dynamics, at the appropriate place in the chapter on the government. Here it is enough to say that while the reforms improved the imperial structure's functional order and rationality, they did not result in greater participation by society, or in the introduction of any constitutional elements. In this respect, they proved a great disappointment to the young elite.

Along with the administrative reforms that were planned or actually implemented, the first years of Alexander's reign also witnessed dramatic progress in the areas of economic and educational policy. We may briefly characterize the new economic orientation as an encouragement of individual enterprise and laissez-faire economics. The state, however, qualified this liberalism by the recognition that it had to help in initiating new large-scale industrial or commercial ventures through subsidies and tariffs, rather than by direct supervision, and that it had the obligation to protect the weak from the impact of innovation. We may view this approach as a natural extension of Catherine's program. The policy gave impetus to an agricultural and industrial expansion whose fruits, however, were not to be reaped until the reign of Nicholas I.

In the realm of education, Alexander created new universities at Kharkov, Kazan, Dorpat (Iur'ev), and St. Petersburg, endowing them —as well as the existing University of Moscow—with a liberal statute that provided for a large degree of academic freedom and autonomy. A plan for a network of secondary schools to cover all Russia was not implemented, although the number of such institutions greatly increased. A number of special educational establishments were opened, among which the best known were the Juridical Institute and the *lycées* at Tsarskoe Selo and Odessa, which offered more and varied educational opportunities to the younger generation and also widened the scope of professional training. Finally, there was a thorough overhaul of the system of ecclesiastical schools. They were given a solid economic foundation, and their curriculum was modernized: Russian instead of Latin was made the language of instruction; the offerings in modern languages and the natural sciences were expanded and improved. The reform did not benefit only the clergy; it had a far-reaching impact on Russian professional and cultural life, since the majority of Russian scholars and scientists in the later years of the nineteenth century were to come from these modernized ecclesiastical schools. Nor should we forget the reform of the military establishment, especially the artillery and technical branches, which made the empire's fighting forces a match for Napoleon's.

Significant as the reforms and transformations of Alexander's early years were to prove to have been in the long run, his reign was actually dominated by the struggle against Napoleonic France and its diplomatic aftermath. No sooner had Alexander I taken the reins of government than he recalled the hapless Cossack corps sent out against India by Paul and came to terms with England. Without going into the intricacies of the diplomatic game, it will be enough to mention that Alexander concluded an alliance with Prussia, to which he was to remain faithful throughout his reign, and then joined in the Third Coalition against France. His troops, along with those of his Austrian allies, met their decisive defeat at Austerlitz (1805). After a brief truce, not sincerely kept by either side, Russia again joined Prussia against Napoleon. The short campaign ended in Prussia's annihilation at Jena and Auerstädt, while the Russian army was defeated at Preussisch-Eylau and Friedland (1806–1807). Alexander decided to come to terms with France and negotiated the peace of Tilsit at his meeting with Napoleon on the Niemen. During the next few years, an uneasy peace was preserved with France. Reluctantly, Russia joined the Continental System devised by Napoleon to strangle England economically. Alexander renewed his alliance with Napoleon at Erfurt in 1809, but the interview between the two emperors made it clear that their collaboration could not long be maintained. Napoleon failed to persuade Alexander to move directly against England, even though he offered to divide the Near East into a Russian and a French sphere of influence. The suggestion of a dynastic alliance through a marriage between Napoleon and a sister of Alexander also failed to materialize. In the end, Russia's unwillingness to apply the Continental System and Alexander's feeling that Napoleon's threat to the system of Europe was too great made conflict inevitable.

In the spring of 1812 Napoleon invaded Russia with an army of over half a million men, three-quarters of which were auxiliary troops furnished by more or less willing European allies and vassals. The outcome of the campaign is well known. Having suffered great losses in his advance on Moscow, Napoleon was forced to turn back when Alexander spurned his overtures for peace and when Moscow was burned. The retreat of the French turned into flight after the crossing of the Berezina River. Despite the loss of almost the entire Grande Armée, Napoleon was able to recover and reconstitute his forces. He was, however, decisively defeated by a new coalition at the Battle of Leipzig (1813). From then on, in spite of temporary successes and holding operations, Napoleon was forced to retreat farther and farther until the allies entered Paris on March 13, 1814. Napoleon then abdicated and went into exile on the island of Elba.

The main architect of Napoleon's defeat, Alexander emerged as the "savior" of Europe, and Russia as the strongest power on the Continent: Alexander accepted Louis XVIII as King of France, but compelled him to grant a constitution, the Charte. While the allies were negotiating the terms of a general peace settlement in Vienna, Napoleon returned from Elba and tried to recover his throne. His attempt ended on June 18, 1815, at Waterloo, and resulted in a second occupation of Paris and Napoleon's definitive banishment to St. Helena. By the final settlement of Vienna (1815), Russia received most of the former kingdom of Poland, on the basis of a personal union. In 1818 Alexander granted Poland a relatively liberal constitution and installed his brother, Constantine, as Viceroy. The Treaty of Vienna also ratified Russia's earlier acquisition of Finland (by the Treaty of Frederiksham, 1809), as well as her protectorate over the

Funeral procession for Field Marshall Kutuzov, victor over Napoleon

Alexander I—in Paris, 1815

principalities of Wallachia and Moldavia which had been secured in 1812 after a war with Turkey. Alexander was the initiator of the Holy Alliance, which pledged its signatories to rule in a benevolent and Christian spirit. Russia was also one of the partners in the Quadruple Alliance, set up to prevent any revolutionary government from coming to power in France and to maintain the political, as well as diplomatic, status quo. As main architect of the new system, and reveling in his role as savior of Europe and Christianity, Alexander became more and more involved in diplomacy. He himself attended the congresses called by the signatories of the Quadru-

Count A. A. Arakcheev

ple Alliance, and began to neglect domestic affairs. Then, having experienced a religious conversion, the emperor was engulfed by the mood of mysticism prevalent at the time. He removed himself more and more from everyday concerns, becoming unaware of the needs and demands of the country.

Alexander of course did not completely ignore domestic problems, but he delegated routine administration to subordinates. Among the latter, A. A. Arakcheev, now a count, became his most influential assistant, carrying out his master's orders with inflexible and brutal energy. The establishment of the military colonies (see the later chapter on social classes) was the most significant attempt at domestic reform in the period. In the opinion of their initiators, the military colonies were to result in a restructuring of the Russian peasantry.

Reality, however, fell far short of these sanguine expectations. The peasants settled in the military colonies were subjected to harsher discipline and worse conditions than they had experienced before; they resented and rebelled against the petty supervision, strict discipline, and military atmosphere that prevailed in the colonies, many of which, in addition, did not have the expected physical amenities because of graft, corruption, and inefficiency on the part of the administrators. Alexander also toyed with schemes for better organization of local government, but they did not have much practical impact. Finally, frightened by the new liberal ideas that had taken root in Europe, and prompted by his own obscurantist mysticism, Alexander revoked the relatively liberal rules of censorship he had issued in 1804 and subjected literary and academic life to extremely rigid and bigoted controls.

The French invasion and the subsequent Russian victory over Napoleon had an exhilarating effect on Russian society. National pride and self-respect rose to a high pitch, and the educated elite felt that the nation's contribution to Napoleon's defeat had given each and every Russian (including the serfs, who also had risen against the invader) a new sense of dignity; the people had earned the right to be treated with respect by the government—like genuine citizens, not subjects. Their disappointment and anger were therefore so much the greater when, after 1815, Alexander introduced strict censorship, obscurantism, harsh police controls, and military colonies.

But the intellectual ferment of the first decade of the nineteenth century could not be stopped. It was invigorated by the impact of war, the contact with Western European patriotic and liberal organizations like the *Tugendbund,* the continuing ties with Western Europe, especially France and England. Finally, the granting of a constitution to Poland; the preservation of Finnish autonomy; the news of the revolutions in Naples, Spain, and South America; and the liberal agitation in Germany and France contributed to a similar ferment and agitation among the elite and youth of Russia. Secret societies were formed to discuss programs of reform. At first, these societies aimed at little more than organizing like-minded young men to participate actively in improving Russian life (for example, to better the lot of their serfs, educate the soldiers under their command, disseminate liberal ideas and useful information through publications and discussion circles). But soon the original associations, patterned on the masonic lodges and the *Tugendbund,* turned toward radicalism and political action. They were no longer content to discuss plans of reform and vague constitutional projects, and began to consider the possibility of carrying out a coup or revolution to seize power and change the regime. They thought that their opportunity had come when Alexander died suddenly in November 1825. Taking advantage of the confusion that accompanied the succession, they attempted a coup on December 14, 1825—hence their name, Decembrists. They failed. Their action, however, not only marked the beginning of a new reign, but that of a new period in Russian history as well—the repressive rule of Nicholas I, which was accompanied by the intellectual, cultural, economic and social gestation of a modern Russia that emerged with the Emancipation and the reforms of the reign of Alexander II.

The Empire

Amodern army and navy were the necessary instruments for the preservation, as well as creation, of the Russian Empire. Recognizing this fact early, Peter I proceeded to shape such a tool even before he had wrested power from his half-sister Sophie. His play regiments were organized, drilled, and equipped with artillery on the pattern that prevailed then in Western Europe. This was the origin of the first regiments of the Guards— Semenovsky, Preobrazhensky—the training ground and pool of much of Russia's military and governmental leadership throughout the eighteenth and early nineteenth centuries. Peter's adolescent play also served to lay the foundation of the navy. But it was obviously the long war against Sweden that helped forge the army and navy into effective instruments of Russian imperial policy. Peter himself acknowledged that the Russians learned the principles of modern military organization and warfare from their enemy, the Swedes. The emperor elaborated on these principles, incorporated the precepts of contemporary German theorists, and in 1716 came up with the Military Statute (Ustav voinskii) that remained the basis for the organization and discipline of the imperial army even beyond the end of our period. It was complemented by a Naval Statute (Ustav morskoi, 1720) that owed much to English precepts.

The military establishment created by Peter was a professional, technically trained fighting force whose officers and men served for most of their lives. It was therefore a permanent professional institution. Coming after what Michael Roberts[1] has so aptly called the military revolution of the seventeenth century, it had all the features associated with the armies of Louvois and Frederick William I of Prussia. There was, however, one notable difference with the prac-

[1] M. Roberts, "The Military Revolution 1560–1660" in *Essays in Swedish History,* London 1967, pp. 195–225.

tice of continental Europe. In the West the recruitment and supplying of most army units were delegated to their colonels who, at
times, were in fact military entrepreneurs, proprietors of their
regiments. Not so in Russia. There from the very beginning the state
exercised complete control; the government alone supplied and
equipped, as well as recruited, the soldiers. Not only was the army
(and navy) under the state's direct supervision and control, but the
supplying and moving of the military units also fell within the
responsibilities of the administrative institutions of the empire. This
situation created one of the most important stimuli for administrative reorganization. At the same time, because it was organized along
rational and functional lines, the military establishment provided a
model and the personnel for a similarly oriented administrative
structure. This was, of course, more particularly the case in frontier
areas, where the army not only provided the defense, but also exercised the basic administrative functions. All this tended to give a
militaristic cast of mind and introduce army ways of operation into
the imperial civil administration as well.

The new military machine laid a heavy burden on the country.
First, soldiers had to be recruited. During the first two-thirds of the

"Peter I"—V. A. Serov, 1907

eighteenth century, one recruit had to be furnished for every 150 males; in the Turkish war of 1768–1774, the quota was raised to one for every 100; and during the struggle against Napoleon, the burden was increased even more, in addition to the calling up of militia. As service lasted for twenty-five years, it was virtually lifelong, for few *European influence on* men managed to survive it. Not only did such a system separate the soldier from his home, family, and village; it also isolated him from Russian society. He became an obedient tool of the state, and in *soldier* addition he also received some veneer of European culture, as far as it was reflected in the military establishment. If garrisoned in provincial centers or, more rarely, if he retired as an "invalid" and was given work in local administrative offices, he served as a conduit for a more rationalistic, "Western" outlook and was a source of information about other ways of life and countries with which he may have had contact in the course of his service. Such a role played by recruits is of course difficult to document, and it is set forth here only as a hypothesis.

In the second place, the new military establishment cost a great deal of money, a fact that was reflected in the budgetary situation of the empire. Curiously enough, however, the share of expenditures for the military in the total budget did decrease after Peter I, although the size and importance of the army did not. It was the cost of government that rose. Naturally, with the onset of the wars against Turkey, and more particularly with the wars against Napoleon in the early nineteenth century, this favorable situation could not be maintained; military expenditures took the lion's share of the budget. Catherine II had to resort to issuing paper money whose volume rapidly expanded under Alexander I, so that there was a parallel decline in its value with respect to silver. Only the long period of relative peace after 1815 permitted Finance Minister Count Kankrin to balance the budget in the reign of Nicholas I. Included in the expenditures for the military establishment was the cost of equipping and arming it—needs usually met from domestic production. The military therefore provided the major impetus to the development of Russian industrial and mining enterprises in the eighteenth and early nineteenth centuries. Imports for military needs were relatively few, and contracts with foreigners to supply the army or navy were usually discouraged by the government for reasons of security and patriotism, even if it meant greater expense. This serves also to explain why the state initiated and administered so many of the earliest industrial enterprises. Established to serve the requirements of the military, the industrial enterprises were often under the supervision of army and navy officers, who naturally introduced concepts of military administration and organization into the economic sector.

Numerically, the Russian military establishment was one of the largest in Europe. But only a portion of the total military contingent met the standards of eighteenth-century military professionalism. A great number of units and contingents were still of the semitrained militia type.[2] The navy played too subordinate a role throughout our period to deserve consideration here. It was important not so much for its military role (with the notable exception of Orlov's Mediterranean expedition during Catherine II's first Turkish war), as for opening up new territories in the Far East and for the administration of Kamchatka and the Pacific shore districts of eastern Siberia. Both the army and navy also ran a number of educational institutions that naturally played a great role in the cultural development of the empire (some aspects of this role will be dealt with in Chapter 7).

Let us briefly review the history of the empire's borders and sketch the methods used in absorbing the new territories and peoples.

By coincidence, the long-drawn-out negotiations with China were brought to a conclusion by the signing of the Treaty of Nerchinsk in the same year in which Peter wrested power from Sophie. By the terms of this treaty, the Russians had to withdraw from the Amur Valley. Thereafter, the border with the Celestial Empire remained unchanged until the middle of the nineteenth century; Russian expansion in Siberia was halted, except for the discovery and occupation of Kamchatka and of Alaska in the mid-eighteenth and early nineteenth centuries. The Treaty of Nerchinsk also regulated commerce between China and Russia: trade was to take place primarily at the border town of Kiakhta; a limited, fixed number of Russian trading caravans was allowed into China proper; and eventually a Russian mission was established in Peking. The ups and downs of trade and diplomatic contacts with China would involve us in too much detail, but it may be worth mentioning that the Peking mission offered an opportunity for training in the Chinese language and for laying the foundation of Russian Sinology and Oriental studies. As for the trade at Kiakhta, it played a role in the economic development and the administration of Siberia, since it stimulated settlement along the highway between the Urals and China (*Bolshoi sibirskii trakt*). In terms of actual economic gain, the China trade was a minor operation; the Russians imported mainly tea, a few

---

[2] According to a report on the composition of the armed forces as of December 12, 1761 (submitted on April 27, 1762)—i.e., during the Seven Years' War—there were 115,514 regular army and 8,375 irregulars abroad (a total of 123,889), and 168,287 regulars and 233,664 irregulars at home (a total of 401,951). The overall total, in the field and in garrisons, was 283,801 regulars and 242,039 irregulars (a total of 525,840). (Ts.G.A.D.A., Fond 203, No. 1 [Memoranda, reports, accounts submitted to Peter III, January–July 1762], fol. 101–6.)

luxury items, and rhubarb. Government monopoly, the difficulties of travel, and the unavailability of Russian products for which there was a significant demand in China made this exchange a somewhat haphazard and peripheral operation. It was only with the settlement of Siberia and the development of private trade in the early nineteenth century that the groundwork could be laid for a change in the pattern, but the dramatic reversal came only in the second half of the nineteenth century.

While the Far Eastern boundaries of the empire remained practically unchanged during the century and a quarter with which we are concerned here, the situation was radically different in the west, the south, and the southeast. The eighteenth century, like the sixteenth and seventeenth, was one of active imperial expansion; this expansion, moreover, took place in areas that historically and socioculturally were quite different from the traditional "frontier" lands of sixteenth-century Muscovy. Let us review these territorial changes not in chronological, but in geographic order. Our focus will be not so much on the actual process of acquisition as on the problems and nature of the pattern of the incorporation of new areas and peoples into the social, economic, and political fabric of the empire.

It may not be superfluous at this point to make explicit a few basic features: Except for the last two decades, our period antedates the rise of modern nationalism, both in Russia and the West. The Russian government never even conceived of such a thing as a "nationality problem" in our modern, post-Romantic, sense. Imperial officials were hardly conscious of Russian "nationalism," although they were very much aware of the All-Russian state, the empire, and possibly of the cultural character and religious mission of its history. *A plus forte raison,* they were blind to the national consciousness and feelings of other peoples. They recognized differences in language and religion, but—with minor exceptions, such as Catholicism and Judaism—considered these to be rather superficial external accidents that need not appreciably influence administrative or social patterns. More significant in their eyes were differences in ways of life—that is, whether a people was settled and tilled the soil, nomadic and raised cattle, or merely engaged in hunting and fishing. Generalizing for the entire period (although this policy was gradually and consciously adopted only in the mid-eighteenth century, made explicit in the reign of Catherine II, and consistently acted upon in the early nineteenth century), we may say that the Russian government aimed at the adoption of one way of life by all peoples of the empire. Not unexpectedly, Russian agricultural society was to serve as the model for the other nationalities. In short, the government's goal was a uniform pattern of administra-

tion throughout the empire, a uniformity which, it was believed, required a single way of life, but not necessarily one language, one religion, or even a single culture on the part of all subjects of the emperor. Officials in the eighteenth century were quite unaware that such a policy might possibly be equated with what later was to be called Russification and provoke the resentment and resistance of the nationalities. It was to be the root of much subsequent misunderstanding and conflict. We shall consider the problems of incorporation in the following order: the Baltic provinces, Finland,

Poland, the Ukraine and the southeast, the Caucasus, the Uralo-Caspian frontier, Siberia. As we move from the northwest to the east, we shall contend with different types of problems and solutions, depending on the social and political character of the territories involved.

The acquisition of the Baltic provinces occurred through military conquest during the Great Northern War against Sweden, and it was ratified by the Treaty of Nystad in 1721 (Courland and part of Livonia were annexed somewhat later). At the time of the conquest, Peter I guaranteed the existing privileges of the towns and nobility in return for their complete submission. The provinces thus retained their traditional social and political structure. The towns—particularly Riga, Reval, Dorpat—were administered by their German-speaking patriciate and bourgeoisie; the countryside, on the other hand, was controlled by a German-speaking nobility. The latter were the so-called Baltic barons—most of whom were descended from members of the military orders that conquered and Christianized the region in the Middle Ages—who lorded over the native peasantry (Latvians and Estonians). In the past there had been numerous sharp conflicts between the patriciate and the landed nobles who had tried to extend their domination to the towns. This system was so totally different from the traditional Russian pattern, especially with respect to the powers of local government of the landowning nobility and the urban patriciate, that it could not be incorporated into the empire without either subverting the Russian tradition or itself being eroded by the latter. The history of the relationship between the Baltic territories and the imperial authorities in the eighteenth century was therefore one of gradual dwindling of local political autonomy in return for the preservation of the economic and social status quo.

After the conquest of the provinces, the imperial government naturally imposed its sovereignty and jurisdiction. The governors and governor-generals appointed by St. Petersburg were guided by the interests and requirements of the empire, which meant that as long as the provinces were exposed to invasion by Sweden, there would be strict control and the mobilization of all resources. The conflict between the municipalities and the provincial administrations, dominated by the landed nobility, provided the Russian officials with many opportunities to intervene and settle the dispute in such a way as to weaken both parties politically and increase the power of the central authorities. While for a long time Riga remained the largest and most active port of the empire, it was in sharp competition with the growing facilities of St. Petersburg, as well as the preference accorded newer ports (those on the Black Sea, for instance, later in the century). Even more important in the long run was the fact that the pattern of Riga's trade (and that of other Baltic harbors) changed completely; instead of being a peripheral outpost of the German Hansa, it became the leading port handling Western imports (from England, Holland) and Russian exports such as naval stores, grain, hemp, flax, lumber. Its economic dependence on the empire grew stronger and stronger, and naturally its municipal affairs came more and more under the control of the imperial bureaucracy. At the same time, it was the imperial administration that protected the municipalities from the landed nobility, and in so doing helped to preserve the dominant economic and cultural role of the German bourgeoisie in the Baltic towns.

Contrary to what is often written in textbooks, the German nobility from the Baltic did not secure a prominent place in the Russian state service immediately after the incorporation of the provinces. As a matter of fact, during most of the eighteenth century, the number of Baltic Germans in high places remained quite small.[3] Baltic nobles continued to study abroad, and they retained the right to serve or not to serve in the imperial army or administration. Unlike their Russian counterparts, the noblemen from Livland, Estonia, and Courland were deeply involved in the management of their estates and the local government of their provinces; for this reason, not as many entered the Russian government establishment as is sometimes believed. Yet it is quite true that a good number did enter the imperial service, where their better education and their knowledge of Western practices helped them to successful, at times even brilliant, careers. It should also be stressed that the Baltic nobles were not overly eager to merge with the Russian nobility; indeed, they wanted to preserve their separateness and traditional privileges against the encroachments of the Russian state. Despite their efforts, however, they could not keep their separate identity intact.

Russian encroachment began with the granting of landed estates (confiscated from or abandoned by the Swedish nobility) to Russian dignitaries. The custom was started by Peter the Great, who gave extensive estates near the new capital to his aides and favorites. The new members of the noble estate in the Baltic provinces had another outlook and a different set of interests, and they did not really become assimilated into the old local nobility. At the same time, however, their presence weakened the latter's traditional customs and scope in local affairs. Local autonomy was further

---

[3] Naturally, this does not take into account the personal favorites of Anna and Peter III. But the best known among the imperial dignitaries with German names in the eighteenth century were not from the Baltic provinces, but from Germany proper: Osterman, Münnich, Bennigsen.

eroded by the fact that appeals had to be addressed to the Russian central institutions which had ultimate jurisdiction in all cases, civil or criminal, that could not be adjudicated on the provincial level. Significantly, the deputies from the Baltic nobility to the Legislative Commission of 1767 were more interested in preserving their separateness and local rights than in helping their fellow nobles in Russia to a similar status. The original intention of Peter III to grant the Russian nobility freedom from service "as in Livland" was quietly dropped from the final text of the manifesto of February 18, 1762. It then became easy for Catherine II to abolish virtually the autonomy of the Baltic nobility, while giving a corporate status and participatory rights in local government to all nobles of the Russian Empire.

As the opportunities for advancement in the Russian service increased in the early nineteenth century, the Baltic nobles joined the establishment, became bicultural (without giving up either their own tongue or their Lutheran religion), and focused their efforts on the preservation of control over their serfs. This aspect of the Baltic situation gave the Russian government an additional lever to keep these nobles down. The peasants of the Baltic provinces were Latvian and Estonian serfs, terribly poor and exploited, who had taken from their masters the externals of Lutheran Christianity and Western medieval civilization. To safeguard its control over the Baltic nobility, the government of St. Petersburg at various times considered schemes to convert the native peasants to Russian Orthodoxy. The Russian Church was allowed to send priests and missionaries to minister to the alleged spiritual needs of the peasants who lived close to the old Muscovite border, among whom there were quite a few communities of Old Believers. Discussions were also held on the desirability of undertaking the education of the serfs, using their native language. These plans naturally encountered the determined opposition of the Baltic ruling classes, who were willing to submit to greater central control over the provincial administration provided that their effective mastery of the native peasantry was not jeopardized. This development culminated in the emancipation of the Baltic serfs by the government of Alexander I (1816–1819), but on terms dictated by the local nobility, that is, without land. The settlement allowed the landowners to retain their economic grip on the peasantry. In return, the Baltic nobility turned into a class of most loyal and efficient servants in the military, civil, and cultural establishments of the empire.[4] It is from this period that the very

---

[4] Under changed conditions, new conflicts arose between the Baltic Germans and the Russian government in the middle of the nineteenth century; this time they led to a policy of enforced Russification.

prominent, although by no means monopolistic, position of the Germans in the Russian bureaucracy dates.

In the general nature of its incorporation, the fate of Finland was related to that of the Baltic provinces. The Grand Duchy of Finland —except for so-called Old Finland (eastern Karelia), which was annexed under Peter I—became Russian by the Treaty of Frederiksham in 1809. This was a consequence not only of Russia's victory over Sweden (under whose rule the province had been until then), but also of an agreement reached between Russian authorities and the local nobility of Swedish origin. At the Diet of Borgo, Alexander I agreed to respect the political system of the Grand Duchy and the rights and privileges of all its classes. Finland was to be united with the Russian Empire in the person of their common sovereign—the Emperor and Grand Duke—although the exact legal nature of the bond remained a subject of controversy. At any rate, Alexander granted anew and solemnly guaranteed the traditional constitution of the Finnish nation. Finland thus became joined to the empire as an autonomous and separate entity, with its own Diet, and system of administration and justice. Rumor had it (and Russian liberal society expected it) that this settlement would serve as model for the reorganization of the empire along federal lines and for the extension of similar "constitutional" guarantees to all imperial subjects. This did not happen; subsequently, rather, but outside the chronological limits of this volume, problems similar to those faced by the Baltic provinces arose in Finland, and the Russian government restricted, and eventually suspended, the constitution of the Grand Duchy.

The incorporation of territories of the former Commonwealth of Poland and Lithuania was the outcome of diplomatic negotiations between the partitioning powers and of the political situation in Europe at the time. We need not retrace the steps that led to the end of Polish independence, nor need we determine the relative share of guilt to be borne by the partitioning rulers, Maria Theresa, Frederick II, and Catherine II. In brief, the treaties of partition, 1772–1795, awarded Russia most of the former Grand Duchy of Lithuania with its Byelorussian possessions and some territories in eastern Poland. The Treaty of Vienna, 1815, gave Alexander I central Poland, with the capital, Warsaw. Russia thus came to control the largest part of that unhappy country.

This acquisition gave rise to two sets of problems resulting from the Russian attitudes with respect to the lands they occupied. The Russians considered the eastern provinces of Poland-Lithuania, particularly those incorporated by the terms of the first partition agreement in 1772, to be genuinely Russian lands—lands that had been originally taken from Moscow's Kievan inheritance by Lithuania in the fifteenth and sixteenth centuries. They were seen as restituted to their rightful sovereign, and this view was reinforced by the fact that the local peasants were Byelorussians (who were equated with the Russians) and Orthodox, while only their landlords were mainly Polish and Catholic. These territories, therefore, were more easily, albeit gradually, assimilated into the normal patterns of Russian administration, justice, and finance. Catherine II was willing to make provision for a transitional stage, but she made it quite clear in her instructions to the governor-general, and he in turn in his proclamations, that total "russification" in an administrative sense was the goal. Eventually these territories were to constitute the Western governorships (Zapadnye gubernii) with the same status as any other central Russian province. On the other hand, the truly Polish lands—the heartland of former Lithuania, Vilna, was considered a special case—were allowed to retain their laws, a separate administration, and their traditional social and political structures. The Russians reserved to themselves only final jurisdiction (exercised as a function of what seemed politically most desirable at a given time), and maintained law and order. Until 1815, the territory enjoying this autonomous status was not very large (it had also been annexed last, 1795, and during this time Russian concern over the wars against France was paramount). Its status did not give rise to serious problems, although it is true that the Russian government could not count on the population's submission or loyalty, as was proven by the formation of a Polish legion which fought for Napoleon until Leipzig.

By the terms of the Treaty of Vienna, Alexander received most of the former Grand Duchy of Warsaw (a puppet state created by Napoleon). Together with other Polish territories acquired earlier, it was constituted into a Kingdom of Poland—the so-called Congress Kingdom—of which the emperor of Russia became the hereditary king on a personal basis. In 1818 Alexander I granted Poland a constitution that guaranteed the separateness and full autonomy of the kingdom; the Polish army, recruited on the basis of a general draft, was separate from the Russian and had its own command headed by the viceroy of Poland, Alexander's brother Constantine. The kingdom had its own Diet, local administration, judiciary, and system of education; the official language was Polish. To what extent Alexander was a good constitutional king of Poland is a moot question. In fact, however, aside from the matter of national independence, the main source of trouble between Russians and Poles was the status of the so-called Western provinces. Pursuing Catherine II's policy of assimilation, N. N. Novosil'tsev, the vicegerent of former

Lithuania, pressed for russification, since in the government's opinion these territories belonged to Russia proper. The opinion was not shared by the Poles, who wanted these lands restored to the Kingdom of Poland. As is well known, the Polish revolution of 1831 resulted in the abrogation of the Constitution of 1818, while the second Polish revolt of 1863 brought about the virtual eradication of Poland as a separate administrative and political entity.

One thing is certain: the partitions incorporated into Russia a populous nation with its own proud history, tradition, and culture, professing a religion which connected it with Rome and other Catholic powers in Europe. It was a foreign element which could neither forgive nor forget that it had been brutally deprived of its national existence, an existence it had enjoyed for centuries with glory and with much success. The Poles could not reconcile themselves to their fate, and they saddled the imperial government with many difficult problems of internal policing. The difficulty was compounded by the government's inability to recognize the factor of national consciousness, for it reacted to the Poles not as members of an alien nation, but as Russian disobedient subjects. Moreover, the necessity of keeping the Poles submissive proved to be a factor in determining Russian foreign policy, a policy that was never free from pressure by Western powers and the need to maintain the "robbers' alliance" with Prussia and Austria.

The consequences of the tensions and conflicts between the Russian government and the Poles occurred in a subsequent period, but it may not be amiss to note at this point that the first partition of Poland also resulted in the incorporation into the empire of a people that previous rulers had been at pains to keep out: the Jews. Thereafter, the Jewish minority remained a permanent factor in the situation of southwestern and western Russia. Again, the major difficulties for the government arose much later. Catherine II did nothing but recognize the existing forms of Jewish community life and keep the Jews out of the central provinces and the capitals (although she did not object to their settling in the provinces of New Russia). The first comprehensive legislation concerning the Jews was drawn up in the early years of the reign of Alexander I. By the terms of the statute of 1804, the Jewish communal institutions (for example, the *kagal*) were given the right to adjudicate and decide all matters relating to their religious beliefs and practices according to their customs. The community and its elected leaders were made responsible to the Russian administration in all cases involving Russians or requiring administrative intervention; in such cases, of course, Russian law was applicable.

Alexander's advisors (as well as the Decembrist leader Paul Pestel) did not believe that it was necessary to change the religious loyalty of the Jews; they aimed rather at breaking down their isolation and exclusiveness. The legislation implementing this point of view was experienced as discriminatory by the Jews. The act of 1804 stipulated that if any Jews wanted to leave their community, they would have the right to do so, provided that they accepted the practices and standards of the Russian population with respect to dress, customary law, and the like. In short, they would obtain equality of status on condition of cultural russification, but not necessarily conversion. This the Jews would not do, and their refusal subsequently provoked Nicholas I to harsh and repressive measures. Again, because of their inability to understand and make allowance for a feeling of national identity (of course, in the case of the Jews it was closely bound up with religion, but was this different from Muslim Tartars?), the imperial officials saw their well-intentioned action rebuffed. In a mood of pique, they resorted to reprisals and discrimination, and in so doing they paved the way for Jewish disaffection in the second half of the nineteenth century.

The assimilation of the southern and southwestern territories presented a more complex picture, for several distinct trends and developments became intertwined. The core of the traditional Ukraine (left bank of the Dnieper and Zaporozh'e), dominated by the Cossacks, had come under Muscovite overlordship in 1654. By the Treaty of Pereiaslavl' in that year, the Cossacks had been promised the preservation of their traditional system of government, of their customs and laws. But soon after the acceptance of Moscow's protectorate, there began the process that was to bring about the disintegration of the traditional social and political patterns of Cossack society. Muscovy largely contributed to it by reneging on the promises made at Pereiaslavl' and by gradually impinging on the autonomy of the region; yet in the final analysis, it was the process of internal social disintegration that played the decisive role in the russification of the Ukraine. Limited to its essentials, this process consisted in the gradual transformation of the elected officers (*starshina*) into a hereditary class; in addition, the members of this new ruling class acquired a disproportionate amount of wealth in land and cattle that enabled them to dominate the rank-and-file Cossacks and peasants politically, as well as economically. It is true that the process had begun before the treaty of 1654, but Moscow fostered and speeded it: the Russian government not only used the *starshina* to maintain its control, but it attracted the Cossack leaders into the tsar's service, rewarding them with gifts, money, estates, and support in the elections.

This development did not take place without serious friction, the more so since it was accompanied by Moscow's increasingly tighter control over the Cossack Host. Nor were all the members of the *starshina* united in their attitude toward Moscow, which took advantage of their old rivalries and feuds. Fearing a total loss of their traditional status, some members of the *starshina* eventually turned against the Russian government. The best known of such a change of heart, and one which had significant consequences, was the "treason" of Hetman Mazepa, who sided with Charles XII against Peter I at the Battle of Poltava. Fearful of Peter's revenge, many Cossacks from the Zaporozhian *Sich* (the headquarters of the Cossack Host) followed Mazepa in requesting the protection of the sultan; they were allowed to settle in Turkish territory on the lower Dnieper. After the death of Peter I, most returned to the *Sich* at the Zaporozh'e. In the meanwhile, however, the Cossack organization had been further weakened and the involvement of the loyal *starshina* in the Russian establishment had gone on at a more rapid pace. Indeed, the new Petrine state offered many opportunities, through the Table of Ranks, to the *starshina* and the Ukrainian landowning class, who often were better educated than the Russians, for there was in the south a tradition of schooling in numerous institutions of learning in Kiev, Poltava, Belhorod, and elsewhere. Members of the Ukrainian elite entered Russian service; many had good careers and received in reward ranks and estates with serfs in Central Russia.

In the meantime, in punishment for Mazepa's defection, the administrative autonomy of the Ukraine had been much curtailed. The office of Cossack Hetman or elected chief was abolished and the territory put under the control of a "Little Russian College" in which Russian officials had the decisive voice. Although Elizabeth restored the Hetmanate, she did it for the benefit of Cyrill Razumovsky, the brother of her favorite, the Ukrainian Cossack singer A. Razumovsky. The restoration of the office was an empty gesture, since Razumovsky preferred to live in St. Petersburg and the Hetman's Council remained under the domination of Russian officials. Finally, Catherine II abolished the Hetmanate altogether and turned "Little Russia" into a governor-generalship; to this post she appointed Field-Marshal P. A. Rumiantsev-Zadunaisky with specific instructions to bring about the administrative and economic russification of the territory; he was to do it tactfully, but firmly. The cities were allowed to retain the Magdeburg Law (medieval German urban codes), but in most other respects the historic (left bank) Ukraine had been completely assimilated into the administrative pattern prevailing in Central Russia at the end of the eighteenth century. The process had been furthered— and to some extent perhaps even caused—by developments that had taken place in the economic and social realms.

To make the recently acquired Ukraine and the open steppes in the east secure from Crimean and Turkish raids, as well as from the encroachments of Polish magnates, the government of Elizabeth embarked on an active program of military colonization. Following a tradition that had been developed on Europe's steppe frontier by the Byzantine, Ottoman, medieval Russian, and (most recently) the Habsburg empires, the Russian government recruited southern Slavs (with a sprinkling of others) to settle in the Ukraine. The settlers were organized into regiments and received tracts of lands, while the recruiters became their officers and were given individual estates and military ranks. Several such regiments were settled in what was called New and Slavonic Serbia (for the colonists were generically known as Serbians) around Bakhmut, Mynhorod, Elizavetgrad. The local peasantry at first had to work the lands granted to the settlers as tenants; by the 1780s, however, they had all been transformed into serfs. The settlement of these foreigners speeded the process of russification. Indeed, the officers of the new regiments had the status of regular members of the Russian military service hierarchy, which secured them titles of nobility. Soon they realized that the most advantageous careers were to be made in the central institutions of the empire, whether military or civil. Their children became officers and officials in the St. Petersburg establishment, sometimes as government officials in the Ukraine, but more frequently as officers in the Guards and regular army. Their service careers allowed them to purchase more land, lord it over their Ukrainian peasants, and acquire settled estates (that is, serfs) in Russia proper. Their loyalties, as well as their interests, depended entirely on the authorities in St. Petersburg (the court and government), from whom they expected further rewards in the form of ranks and lands.

It may be noted that from a military and economic point of view, this policy of military colonization proved to be less than successful. Most of the colonists turned out to be poor as landowners and mediocre as officers besides; settling them also cost the treasury a great deal. The policy was soon abandoned, but the social transformation it had initiated did not stop. The foreign colonists did not share the Ukrainian elite's nostalgia for the Cossack past, so that they easily became carriers of the values and policies of the Petrine empire. Gradually they also established matrimonial connections with the old *starshina* who had retained wealth and social prestige, and so further contributed to the russification of the Ukrainian upper class and to drawing its members into Russian service. These developments took place at the expense of the traditional patterns of local autonomy and of the non-serf character of agrarian relations in the Ukraine. Both the *starshina* and the new colonists eventually

Control of serfs

secured full mastery over the peasants. The Russian government ratified the *fait accompli* by extending serfdom to the left-bank Ukraine, 1783, and permitting the resettlement in the Ukraine of serfs from estates in Central Russia.

A few words will suffice to deal with the remaining history of the Dnieper Cossack Host. After the flight of a part of the Zaporozhian Host to Turkey, those remaining at the *Sich* were quite powerless and had to submit to the dictates of the Russian government. They were forced to accept strict control over their membership, as well as Russian supervision of their activities (this, too, contributed to many *starshinas* seeking careers in Russia and acquiring estates outside the Cossack territory). The control and supervision did not decrease when those Cossacks who had gone to Turkey decided to return. Internal dissensions, especially conflicts between the rank-and-file and the *starshina* over economic and political matters, kept the *Sich* in ferment. The participation of rank-and-file Cossacks in the administration of the Host was rapidly dwindling, while their pauperization and exploitation by the *starshina* were growing apace. Unrest and rebellions became endemic in the 1760s and 1770s; on the eve of the Pugachev rebellion, a revolt of the lower strata of Cossacks (the *koliivshchina*) severely shook the Host and seriously worried the government. It therefore came as no surprise when, frightened by the Pugachev revolt, Catherine II abolished the *Sich* in 1775. She justified her action by pointing to the unruly and backward character of this military society. The Cossack organization had come to an end on the Dnieper. Some minor and isolated features of it did survive, but more as sentimental folklore (to be exploited by Gogol) than as meaningful elements of a living social pattern.

The Dnieper Cossacks at the Zaporozhian *Sich* had been the original and most important Host, but in the eighteenth century they were no longer the only one. The Don Cossacks had formed their Host on the lower Don in the sixteenth century, and in the eighteenth century they served as the empire's most important bulwark against the Crimea, the Caucasus, and the southeastern steppes. In turn, the Don Cossacks had established the Ural (Iaik) Host on the Iaik (Ural) River, where they engaged in fishing and guarded the steppe frontier against Kalmyk and Bashkir nomads. A Volga Cossack Host had been organized in 1732 to protect the empire against attack from the Caucasian peoples. Both Volga and Don Cossacks furnished the membership of the Black Sea and Kuban Hosts that were created at the end of the eighteenth century. Finally, there were also small Cossack units in Siberia, on the border with the Kirghiz steppe, and for escort and messenger duty along the Siberian trek. These Siberian Cossacks were to become the major constituent element of the Amur and Turkestan Hosts organized in the nineteenth century. As this sketchy enumeration has indicated, the Cossack organization underwent a fundamental change in the course of the eighteenth century: from a particular form of society—a kind of military democracy enjoying a large degree of local autonomy—it was gradually changed into a permanent military formation. In the nineteenth century the Cossacks were merely soldiers (primarily cavalry) who had to be always on call with their own horses and equipment, but who cultivated their land (or engaged in fishing); they lived in settlements (*stanitsy*) whose administrative organization had retained traditional forms, but lost its original autonomous function. The Cossacks were free men, not serfs, they owned their land (both communally and individually) and received privileged treatment as an elite combat force. As such, they played an important role in the imperial military establishment, primarily in the protection of the far-flung eastern borders. As must have become evident from their geographic distribution, they followed the extension of the empire's frontier into the territory of the nomads.

But to return to the eighteenth century. The Don, Ural, and Volga Hosts underwent an internal evolution similar to that experienced by the Dnieper Cossacks earlier. The *starshina* (officers), becoming richer and succeeding in making their status well-nigh hereditary, looked to St. Petersburg, hoping for careers in the capital and willing to act as agents of the central government in their Host's territory. They acquired wealth, mainly in land, on which they proceeded to settle serfs. Culturally, they emulated the way of life of the Russian nobility, sending their children to schools, corps of cadets, and preparing them for careers in the capital and at court. Conflicts developed between the *starshina* and the rank-and-file Cossacks, whose economic lot was hardly enviable, burdened as they were with heavy service obligations and taxes. The friction within the Hosts created an atmosphere of tension and insecurity that manifested itself in revolts, in flights of Cossacks beyond the border (Pugachev was at one time thinking of doing this), in intrigues with other social or national groups. The abrogation of the election of the hetman in favor of appointment exacerbated the situation. After several serious revolts of the Don and Iaik Hosts—the latter also took part in the Pugachev rebellion—Catherine II imposed a definitive reorganization in 1775 on the advice of G. A. Potemkin.[5] The Cossack Host became

[5] To punish them for their leading role in the Pugachev rebellion, the very name of the Iaik river and Cossacks was obliterated by Catherine II and changed to Ural Cossacks and river. The membership of the Ural Host was also sharply curtailed.

a part of the regular military establishment of the empire. Its officers, appointed by the crown, were given the status of Russian officers and noblemen. The hetman, nominated by the sovereign, was to be assisted by a council in which appointed Russian officials were in the majority. In return, the Cossacks were guaranteed respect for their traditional customary law and self-government on the village (*stanitsa*) level, as well as the possession of their land and the exclusion of serfdom from it. This settlement was subsequently extended to all the new Cossack units organized in the nineteenth century.

The process of assimilating the Cossacks was facilitated and hastened by Russia's acquisition of the northern shore of the Black Sea and of the Crimea, as well as by the colonization policy pursued by Potemkin in New Russia, as these newly annexed territories were called. A few remarks on the style of Potemkin's imperial policy may be in order. The Treaty of Kuchuk Kainardji had established an independent khanate of the Crimea. Internal difficulties in the khanate offered the Russians an opportunity to interfere in local and dynastic disputes, and to prepare the takeover of the peninsula. This the Russians did by playing on the national and religious diversity of the population. While the Muslims, mostly Tartars, constituted the majority and provided the ruling elite, there were sizable Christian minorities of Georgians, Armenians, and Greeks. These minorities were a particularly active element in the economic life of the peninsula. The Greeks controlled the maritime trade with Constantinople, while the Georgians and Armenians were efficient and productive truck gardeners on whom the prosperity of the peninsula heavily depended. By blandishments, promises, threats, or outright bribery, the Russians brought about either the expulsion (of some Greeks) or the migration (of Greeks, Georgians, Armenians) from the Crimea. The latter were resettled along the Black Sea shore and in the newly founded cities of Mariupol, Taganrog, and Odessa, where they contributed greatly to the agricultural and commercial development of the region as well as to the cultural life of its rapidly growing cities, especially Odessa. The departure of these minorities undermined the economy and stability of the Crimea, making it an easy prey. The Russians took advantage of dissensions within the ruling family, the Gireis, and occupied the peninsula, but they were careful not to upset the traditional life style of the Crimean Tartars.

The Russian military commandant, who was also the governor, exercised overall control. The routine operations of administration and justice, the collection of taxes, the census, and so forth, remained in the hands of local chieftains and headmen. The Tartar elite was given the opportunity of joining Russian service officially, and in fact many took advantage of their local functions and did so. Their children could receive a Russian education, and russification would follow. The imperial government awarded the lands abandoned by those Tartars who preferred to emigrate to Turkey (as well as the lands previously abandoned by the Christians) to officers and officials serving in the Crimea. Lands were also subsequently sold to Russian nobles who were allowed to settle their Russian serfs on them. In this manner, there developed a new Russian land- and serf-owning elite in the Crimea, a class that also attracted into its ranks those of the native nobility who had become russified. Once the social system on the peninsula had become identical to that of Russia proper, there was no need for administrative separateness. In the beginning of the nineteenth century, the remnants of Crimean autonomy were swept away; it became a regular Russian province with the same institutions and social composition as the heartland of the empire. The Muslims retained some of their traditional customs and ways in matters of religion and on the village level, but these were only the lowliest of peasants who were virtually serfs. Therefore, the annexation also had as one of its consequences the isolation of the Muslim peasantry from both the Russian newcomers and their own traditional elite. It served to pave the way for the particular pattern of nationalist revival and political opposition that emerged at the end of the nineteenth century.

It was not enough to acquire new lands that were still empty, since until the Russian conquest they had been exposed to raids that rendered them quite unsafe for agricultural settlement. It was necessary to make the new acquisitions productive, to extract from their soil all it could yield. This policy was dictated not only by political and military considerations, but also by Catherine II's principle of maximizing all the human and material resources of the empire. In this respect, too, Potemkin laid the foundations for what was to be realized in the first quarter of the next century, although at the time of his death (1791), many of his schemes were in fact utopian and poorly thought through. He, like his imperial mistress, often mistook the glitter of appearance and the acclaim of a servile domestic and foreign public for genuine accomplishment. His efforts were first directed toward settling more people on those newly acquired lands whose future looked most promising—those that were fertile, well served by a river system, and close to the sea. Unlike her predecessor, Catherine did not stress military colonization; rather, she endeavored to settle knowledgeable and experienced farmers who could also serve as models for her Russian subjects in improving and expanding the empire's agriculture. We have mentioned the migration of Christians from the Crimea. German colonists were invited and settled on the Don and the lower Volga. In the long run, they were to contribute greatly to the development of specialized crops; but at first they were not always successful, for many were not prepared for the task in unfamiliar surroundings. Colonists also came from the Baltic and from Sweden. Contrary to the usual practice of the imperial government, even Jews were permitted to settle on the left bank of the Dnieper, provided that they engaged in agriculture.

It was, however, not the foreigners who proved to be most significant in settling and developing the new territories. Numerically, as well as socially, the Russians were the dominant group. The government expended much effort to lure back congregations of Old Believers from Poland, Moldavia, and Turkey where they had fled to escape the persecutions of Peter I, Anna, and Elizabeth. They were promised the unhindered use of their rituals and prayerbooks, and they were exempted from the double capitation normally imposed on Old Believers in the empire. Many returned, but the government's promises were not all kept, for the local bishops refused to abide by the regulations on the use of Old Believer liturgy and books. Russian peasants from the central provinces were settled in the south too. Some came voluntarily; these were the state peasants who had been attracted by the many advantages, including the right to enroll as tradesmen (meshchane) and merchants if they proved moderately successful in this kind of occupation. Finally, private owners were encouraged to resettle their serfs on estates and lands they acquired (or were granted) in the south. Unfortunately, this resulted in the introduction of serfdom to the new areas and the promotion of social uniformity based on bondage throughout European Russia. It also serves to illustrate the paradox of the imperial government's practice with respect to economic and social policy: the use of servile labor and compulsion to bolster economic freedom and social progress.

In a manner that was typical of eighteenth-century rationalism and enlightenment, Potemkin also promoted urban development. He founded new cities—Nikolaev, Mariupol, Kherson, and Ekaterinoslav, the latter serving as capital of the governor-generalship of New Russia. Not only did Potemkin found towns, he endeavored to turn them into important cultural and commercial centers overnight. Ambitious and utopian plans were drawn up for the cities with universities, academies of fine arts and music, museums. Even though most of these extravagant schemes failed to materialize, the cities themselves (especially Taganrog, Mariupol, Ekaterinoslav) thrived, contributing to the rapid expansion of Russian trade in the Black Sea. A dynamic cosmopolitan cultural life soon developed in the

new centers, where Greeks and other settlers from the Mediterranean served as an active and stimulating element. Potemkin further encouraged cultural life in the south by establishing printing presses, founding newspapers, and opening several secondary schools. All in all, within one generation, the south of Russia (especially Odessa) rivaled the central provinces of the empire economically and culturally.

Catherine II also prepared, or rather fortified, the base from which Russia penetrated into the Caucasus in the first half of the nineteenth century. Following the annexation of the Crimea, Potemkin secured strategic areas in Kabardinia and Abkhazia by extending a protectorate over local Christian princelings. The really significant advance into the Caucasus, however, occurred when the king of Georgia, hard-pressed by his Muslim neighbors, who were supported by Turkey, asked the Russian emperor for protection. In 1801 the last king of Georgia moved to Russia, and the country was incorporated into the empire (not without some pressure from Russia, to be sure). The annexation of Georgia paved the way for Russia's involvement in the confused situation in Transcaucasia; it marked the beginning of a series of lengthy campaigns that only ended on the eve of the Crimean War with the defeat of the resistance to Russian conquest led by Shamil. It may be noted that the technique of Russian penetration into the Caucasus was the traditional one of exploiting internal dissensions among the native peoples—their mutual hatreds and religious differences. In the first stage of the conquest or annexation, the Russian authorities took care to preserve as much of the social customs and administrative autonomy as possible. But as the conquest was consolidated, as Russian settlers were brought in, as elements within the native elites accepted russification, the special arrangements were abrogated, and the new conquests received the same administrative, judicial (with some qualifications), and economic institutions as the core lands of the empire. In the case of the Caucasus, however, this story belongs to a later period.

Russia's oldest territorial acquisition outside the area of Slavic settlement was the middle and lower valley of the Volga, which came under Moscow's domination in the sixteenth century. Its administrative and economic incorporation had taken place long before the reign of Peter the Great, and in the eighteenth century the area had the same institutions as the central Russian provinces, except for a fairly large number of non-Russian, non-Christian peoples (the Tartars of Kazan, the Cheremiss, the Mordva, and others). The story of the attempts at their conversion belongs to another chapter. But in the reign of Catherine II the first steps were taken in an effort to russify the Tartars. This was not done out of religious considerations, but rather out of a belief—characteristic of the eighteenth-century enlightenment—in the basic uniformity of the higher levels of civilization. This higher civilization, in the opinion of Catherine II and her advisors, rested on settled agriculture and commercial pursuits, and rejected all popular superstitions and traditions not founded on reason. Naturally, the Tartar way of life, based as it was on the Koran, and with its own norms of justice, did not fit the standards elaborated by the enlightened government of St. Petersburg. Without violence, gradually, but systematically, the Russian administration proceeded to eliminate what remained of the traditional Tartar ways; it hoped eventually to do the same with all the Muslims.

While the Volga valley was an old acquisition, this was not the case for the areas east of it, the southern slopes of the Ural mountains and the steppes beyond the Ural River. Largely inhabited by Bashkirs engaged in the raising of cattle and in fishing and hunting, this territory had begun to be penetrated by the Russians in the latter part of the seventeenth century. It had become the object of systematic conquest and occupation only since the reign of Peter I. Russian penetration had started in the traditional manner, ostensibly to protect the Russian settlers east of the Volga from nomad raids. At first, the infiltration had gone almost unnoticed, as local officials concluded defensive agreements and treaties of alliance with clan chiefs to secure Russian interests and to take advantage of the quarrels and rivalries among the various tribes and peoples. These agreements provided the Russian government with ready pretexts for further intervention to secure a firm foothold. In the fluid frontier region, officials seized every opportunity to weaken the native tribes, to acquire more territory, and to displace nomads from the most desirable lands and river systems. As the pressure became obvious and strong, the natives came to realize the extent of Russian penetration and power—but by then they were too weak, divided, and ill-equipped to resist successfully. Russian occupation had become a _fait accompli_, usually symbolized by the building of a fortress which also served as headquarters for the Russian administration and military command of the region.

This is what happened in Bashkiriia, where the talented Russian colonial administrator I. I. Nepliuev secured a firm foothold and then built the fortress of Orenburg on the Ural River (1735/1743). He and his successors then imposed service obligations on the Bashkirs (as frontier guards and auxiliary troops against the Turks) and levied large quantities of horses. The Bashkirs also had to pay tribute, _iassak_, and eventually they were forced to purchase salt at fixed prices from state stores. But even more important in paving the way for the complete incorporation of the area into the empire was the double pressure—social and economic—applied to the nomadic Bashkirs. On the one hand, the Russian administration brought in more Russian agricultural settlers and promoted the expansion of the Ural mining and iron smelting industries. Large tracts of land that were used by the Bashkirs for pasture, as well as the forests and streams in the mountains, fell victim to Russian land hunger. The Bashkirs were forced to sell or exchange much of their land on disadvantageous terms; a great deal of land, especially forests and river banks, was simply seized by the Russians, and the Bashkirs were unable to obtain either compensation or redress. Rather than fight or stay in contact with an alien society, many Bashkirs moved further east, abandoning their lands, pastures, and forests.

At the same time, the Russian government tried to change the Bashkir way of life by converting them to settled agriculture—a higher form of civilization that would result in greater economic benefit to the state, as well as in social and administrative uniformity. Bashkir elders and clan chiefs were promised various rewards—ranks, money, gifts, medals—if they would lead their people in this social and economic transformation. These efforts had some success; a few of the chieftains and their clans turned to agriculture. But in the process a great deal of division and friction arose within Bashkir society. Furthermore, the new tillers of the soil needed additional labor, and they turned to various non-Russian peoples and tribes who settled among the Bashkirs as virtual serfs, the so-called *tepteri*. The object of brutal exploitation as well as social and cultural scorn on the part of the Bashkirs, the *tepteri* became an important source of unrest in native society. Little wonder that these pressures and transformations led to violence and revolt. In the course of the eighteenth century, the Bashkirs revolted repeatedly (in 1735–1741, 1755–1757), and joined the Pugachev rebellion in 1773–1774. In every instance the struggle was long and bitter. Of course, the Bashkirs succumbed to Russian superiority in armament, leadership, and resources. Every defeat brought in its wake repression, increased fiscal burdens, and tighter administrative control.

While the Bashkirs were completely broken and subdued in the aftermath of the Pugachev rebellion, their nomadic neighbors further east and southeast—the Kirghiz, the Kalmyks—remained restless. Russian authority in these areas was nominal rather than real. The process of establishing imperial administrative control over them was so similar to that in the case of the Bashkirs that there is no need to repeat the description. Russian control over the vast steppes east and northeast of the Caspian Sea remained superficial for a long time; no serious efforts at agricultural settlement were made. Inadequate as it was, the Russian presence served to shield the imperial territory from neighboring khanates. Eventually, it also provided a stepping-stone for the conquest of Central Asia in the second half of the nineteenth century.

Last, but not least, we must consider the largest "colonial" domain of the Russian state, Siberia. This subcontinent extends from the Urals to the Pacific Ocean, and in our period the following territories were considered to belong to it economically or administratively:

Kamchatka (discovered and annexed in the eighteenth century), the Aleutian Islands, the Russian settlements on the American continent in Alaska and in northern California (of course, in America only Alaska remained a Russian possession until 1867, when it was sold to the United States). As is well known, the conquest of Siberia was very gradual. It consisted in first establishing control over key river points to secure the main route from Europe. From and around these points agricultural settlements would eventually spread. But throughout most of our period, these settlements remained quite sparse, concentrated in western Siberia, around Tiumen' and To-bol'sk. It was only at the very end of the eighteenth century, in application of Paul's decree of 1799, that an effort was made to settle a large number of peasants near Irkutsk in Transbaikaliia. The effort was only mildly successful. Some industrial settlements, too, had been established near the mines of Kolivan', Voznesensk, and Nerchinsk. Naturally, the border and trading post with China at Kiakhta, as well as the fortress of Semipalatinsk and the important stations on the Siberian trek (Omsk, Irkutsk), had also developed into urban centers. Essentially, however, Siberia was still very much empty territory.

This fact served to condition the government's attitude toward Siberia and its administration. As a local historian put it in the nineteenth century, Siberia was like the far-away estate of a very rich landowner; it furnished only a few special exotic products which, however, did not contribute materially to his revenue. Such a possession, therefore, could be left pretty much alone; it sufficed to see to it that it remained under one's control. And so it was with Siberia throughout the seventeenth century and most of the eighteenth century as well. It was valued mainly as a source of furs. The fur trade had been a state monopoly in the seventeenth century, for it was important in Moscow's foreign policy, since furs were mostly used as gifts to foreign potentates. But in the eighteenth century the value of furs declined sharply, because of Canadian competition, the exhaustion of the best supply in Siberia, and a change in fashion. Peter and his successors turned their attention to Siberia's mining riches, but great distances and the difficulties of exploitation (convict labor had to be used) prevented them from being profitable and contributing significantly to the national economy. Perhaps Siberia's greatest asset was its contact with China. The China trade, fitful and inadequate as it was, proved valuable to the Russians, supplying them with rhubarb, tea, and luxury goods. In the second half of the eighteenth century it became quite apparent to the Russian government that, in order to be genuinely profitable, this trade had to be a two-way affair, with Russian products going to China as well.[6] In view of the distances involved, this necessitated the development of Siberia's population and agricultural potential. The idea took hold firmly in St. Petersburg at the end of the eighteenth century, and led to the plan of 1799 to colonize Transbaikaliia.

In view of Siberia's limited economic role, it is not surprising that its administration was also neglected. In the seventeenth century the most important task of Siberian administrators was to control the roads of access and exit through the Urals, to make sure that there were no violations of the tsar's monopoly of the fur trade. The system had not changed much by the early part of the next century. The governors sent to Siberia were well-nigh absolute there; they took advantage of their position to fill their pockets in complete disregard of the needs of the region and its population, and even of the Treasury. Such practices led a Governor, Prince M. Gagarin, to the scaffold in Peter I's reign. In the course of the century, the regular Russian administrative system—in skeleton form—was extended to Siberia; but, poorly supervised and ill-adapted to the region, it did not prove efficient. The lack of genuine concern or understanding of the special needs of Siberia may be illustrated by the fact that Catherine II ordered the application to Siberia of the statute of 1775, including election of local officials from among the nobility, without even considering that there were no nobles in Siberia and that a crucial aspect of the legislation was inapplicable. Yet, it was this same Catherine who brought about a significant change in the government's attitude toward Siberia. She spoke of Siberia as "our Mexico and Peru," whose potential needed to be developed; this required that greater attention be given to the administration of the region. During her reign several governors and inspectors gathered information that clearly showed the main task of government in Siberia to be the stimulation of economic activity and commerce.

This information was taken quite literally by Governor-general I. B. Pestel, who was appointed in 1805. With the help of energetic subordinates, Pestel proceeded ruthlessly on the principle that all initiative and direction—as well as supervision—had to come from the bureaucracy. The governor brushed aside the only other group that was (and had been in the past) an active agent of economic

[6] It was also hoped that Russia could act as middleman between China and Western Europe. The hope was dashed by the development of maritime trade with China, e.g., the China Clipper trade from New England in the early nineteenth century.

development, the merchants. Pestel not only disregarded their cooperation but also laid the major burden of bureaucratic control on them, exacting vast amounts of money and regulating their activities in petty detail. That this policy was not unaccompanied by graft and corruption, and extraordinary abuse of power, needs no elaboration at this point. Under Russian—and more particularly Siberian—conditions, the systematic imposition of bureaucratic guidance and controls was bound to result in extortion and exploitation of the common people. Far from promoting the economic development of Siberia, the regime of Pestel stifled and impoverished those who would have had the means and skills of entrepreneurial initiative. A radical reform was in order in the subcontinent. It was the work of M. M. Speransky, who was appointed governor-general in 1819; he studied the region until 1821, and in 1822 he had Alexander I promulgate a series of statutes that provided the basic framework of Siberian administration until the end of the century.

Essentially, the effect of the reforms of 1822 was to integrate Siberia more fully into the life of European Russia, although taking into account its special conditions. In so doing, the legislation helped to provide the local population (mainly peasants and merchants) with the security and freedom necessary to enable them to pursue their economic occupations undisturbed by excessive exactions and stifling bureaucratic controls. This is not the place to give a detailed description of the administrative pattern that emerged from Speransky's pen. The following few remarks may suffice to characterize it: Taking into account the vastness of the region, it was subdivided into two governor-generalships, each in turn containing several provinces and special regions under its supervision. The administration of the provinces was organized along functional lines, with a clear demarcation of areas of competence and, what was of particular importance in Siberia, adequate means for the supervision of local officials and for redress in case of need. Account was also taken of the underdeveloped nature of much of the territory and the prospect of its future progress. Thus, a number of regions received only an embryonic administrative organization so as not to burden them unduly with bureaucracy; but as a region's population and productivity increased and it became more integrated into the economy of the empire, its special status was to be replaced by a regular administration and judiciary. The organization of Siberia was patterned on that of the Central provinces to foster the social and economic integration of the subcontinent with European Russia. It was also designed to facilitate agrarian colonization through large-scale and orderly migration of peasants from the over-

19th C. intro. to Marxism broke — AND INDUSTRIALISATION this belief in evolutionary development

populated districts in Central Russia.[7] The goal of the acts of 1822 was therefore the economic, social, and administrative russification of Siberia; and as far as the population of Russian origin was concerned, the legislation succeeded fairly well.

Speransky was quite aware that there were also non-Russian peoples in Siberia, with different ways of life and levels of culture. Although their numbers were not very large, they, too, needed to be well administered, for under proper conditions they could contribute much to Siberia's development. Faithful to his eighteenth-century spiritual heritage, Speransky believed that administration should take into consideration local circumstances and differences, while at the same time promoting gradual russification, so as to bring about an institutional uniformity based on a common way of life. Speransky shared with Catherine II (and the *philosophes*) the notion of social progress determined by an evolutionary development of the way of life from nomad to agriculturist. It was therefore desirable that every nation and people attain the highest stage—settled agriculture and trade; and it was the task of the government to foster and direct this evolution. But Speransky had also fully incorporated the post-Enlightenment notion of each people's or nation's individuality, so that in every case the social evolution, too, was determined by its particular characteristics and physiognomy.

nationalities

The legislation that Speransky devised for the natives of Siberia reflected these two basic points of view. This meant, in short, that the ultimate goal was the russification of most of the natives, but it was to be reached while respecting their traditions and customs, changing their way of life only gradually and on a voluntary basis. The natives of Siberia were divided into several categories, depending on the "level" of their way of life. Those on the highest level, that is, cattle raisers who had begun to be interested in settling and taking up agriculture (for example, the Buriats) were given an administration of some complexity which was almost identical with that of the Russians and which furthered their contacts with the Russian population and administration. Within the clan or village, however, the old traditions could be preserved and internal disputes settled on the basis of customary law. The native chieftains, entrusted with delegated administrative functions, were encouraged to accept russification by learning the language and becoming familiar with Russian culture. Further integration was to be brought about through appropriate encouragement, rewards, free educa-

---

[7] This did not take place right away. Kiselev's reform of the state peasants resulted in a first orderly wave of mass migration, but only the building of the Trans-Siberian Railroad brought about a tidal wave of peasant migrants from central and southern Russia.

tional opportunities for their children, and the like. Natives at a lower level of culture were given simpler administrative structures, and since they were isolated from the mainstream of Siberian life, they had more freedom to preserve their traditional ways. The regular Siberian administration and its officials were not to interfere in village affairs and had to protect the natives from exploitation by merchants and Russian peasants. Again, the local administration was to encourage and reward members of the native elites who took the lead in changing the way of life of their people.

Naturally, the success of the reforms of 1822 would very much depend on their implementation and on the speed with which Siberia could be settled by peasants and its agriculture and trade expanded. But the essential principles of the legislation, foreshadowed, as we have seen, by Catherine's economic policy, as well as by the arrangements made with the peoples of the Crimea and the Caucasus, helped to regularize administrative control over the natives while protecting them from direct competition with higher civilizations and more aggressive peoples. In a wider sense still, the statute for the Siberian natives illustrated the general direction of imperial policy with respect to the non-Russian nationalities: it gave no recognition to national consciousness or to the idea of nationalism; it enunciated as its ultimate goal uniformity in the way of life of all subjects of the empire, a goal that carried a strong implication of cultural russification (for except in the West, Russian civilization was not only that of the dominant society, but also more advanced and attractive). The policy expressed a preference for a gradual and peaceful approach, through example and a change in economic environment, rather than through direct dictate by the government. Ironically, perhaps, this policy served to stimulate the rise of national feeling; and once the latter had become a significant political force, the policy was bound to be resisted and rejected by the nationalities.

[As long as the Russian state did not change its fundamental outlook and the policies based on it, a clash was inevitable between the imperial government and the nationalities. This was demonstrated at the end of the nineteenth century and, in the case of Siberia, quite dramatically at the time of the Revolution. The Russian state proved to have been better equipped for building up a multinational empire than for transforming it into a community of nations and cultures. To a large extent, the cause for this lay in the fact that the principal methods and attitudes of the imperial regime were worked out in the eighteenth century, within an intellectual framework of rationalistic enlightenment, centralistic uniformity, and active government leadership.]

3

The Government

Peter the Great provided the Russian Empire with a framework of political and administrative institutions that remained essentially the same to the end of the imperial regime itself. Of course, individual institutions, their relative importance and their function, did change; but their basic outline and the fundamental conception of the task of administration did not. Peter I did not erect the institutional structure overnight; yet it was not entirely the product of careful analysis and comprehensive planning, either. The new institutions emerged in the heat of war, in answer to great pressures for money, equipment, and personnel that were brought about by the early defeats and the protracted struggle. Only after about 1718 could Peter and his helpmates stop long enough to plan and implement comprehensive changes. But Russian reality and the lessons of experience—which Peter never disregarded—forced basic adjustments in the original setups and shifts of attitudes that on occasion resulted in contradictory solutions. Peter was a pragmatist, a doer rather than a thinker; there can be no question in his case of a purposeful and consistent carrying out of a neat blueprint. This does not mean, however, that his institutional reforms were haphazard, that there was no general concept or mental set that gave direction to all legislative experimentation and action. Peter wanted Russia to become and remain a powerful empire, with a military and economic foundation that would enable her to deal on a footing of equality with other major European states. The old Muscovite system he found wanting because it was cumbersome, inefficient, not professionalized and rationalized enough.

As the emperor was endeavoring to emulate the West, it was to Western Europe that he looked for inspiration, advice, experience, and models. But the political practices of the contemporary European monarchies were dominated by a rationalistic and mercantilocameralistic outlook whose aim was to transform the medieval institutional heritage into an orderly, functional system of administration that would enable the secular state to mobilize its resources and power with maximum effectiveness. Naturally, the carry-overs of traditional habits of mind and of methods, as well as material limitations, precluded a total functional rationalization of administrative machinery. In this respect Peter was at an advantage: he could be more ruthless and reject consciously, systematically, and radically the traditional ways. Furthermore, he had the benefit of contending with a relatively simpler social system in which neither particular groups nor estates had managed to acquire, or retain, the power of effective resistance. For example, the Church was completely dependent on the state, particularly after the fall of Patriarch Nikon, and could not resist the monarch's will. Neither did the service nobility have the local basis of strength and tradition of authority that enabled the nobilities of feudal origin (including the Prussian Junkers) to offer strong resistance to the centralizing monarchy and its "commissars." This obviously does not mean that Peter could disregard tradition, Muscovite experience, and existing institutions altogether. His reign had been preceded by a gradual evolution toward secularization and more orderly (functional) administration; he could, and indeed did, build on its results. The emperor, however, broke more radically with traditional forms than his Western European counterparts had done in the sixteenth and seventeenth centuries—even if in the long run some basic elements proved to have survived. A change in form may, after all, be of great and lasting import. Last, but not least, in politics as in music, *c'est le ton qui fait la musique*—and the "tone" of Peter's actions and plans, his style of government, was totally different from what had been heard in Muscovy before.

However energetic, talented, and ruthless Peter may have been, he obviously could not have done everything himself. He could not have succeeded if he had been actively and consistently opposed by the vast majority of the "ruling class," or even by a significantly large segment of the old elite. It is still one of the unanswered questions of his reign: Who among the traditional service class of Muscovy did, by and large, cooperate with Peter? and why and to what extent did they do so? Was it for lack of choice, out of weakness and passivity? No doubt there was some of that. Were the traditional servitors of the tsars completely dislodged in favor of new men or other classes and estates? Definitely not. It was the old families who furnished Peter's loyal lieutenants and assistants, both on the highest level and in subordinate positions. Were then most members of the "ruling class" themselves in full accord with Peter's new aims and practices? Perhaps it would seem so. But the question remains, why? And so far we have no clear answer.[1]

The basic principles of the Petrine government were simply these: functional organization of administrative institutions (although it could not be completely carried out in practice), hierarchical subordination, orderly (that is, public and clear) procedures. The purpose of the machinery of state was to bring about the fullest mobilization of the empire's resources and to provide leadership for the military, economic, and cultural progress of the nation—all for the greater power and glory of the country and its sovereign. The fullest statement of the principles, with minute details on the procedures to be followed by government offices, was given in the General Regulation (General'nyi reglament, 1720) which spelled out the positive and wide-ranging scope of state action in national life. In addition, as a logical corollary of the active function of the state, the regulation asserted that government should be a government by orderly institutions, not by men. The aspects of personal relationships and authority that characterized patrimonial and patriarchal polities were to be eliminated. The state should exist of and for itself; its officers (including the monarch) were to be its servants; the people, the object of its actions and concerns. This last point must be qualified, for as long as the monarch remained an autocrat, the ultimate arbiter and source of law, he willy-nilly retained elements of personal charisma and aspects of traditional medieval sovereignty.[2] With the death of Alexander I, however, and despite the impressive personal presence of Nicholas I, there disappeared the last monarch to possess and display features of the personal charisma of sovereign power.

Let us list the concrete institutional transformations and innovations introduced by the first Russian emperor. The various areas of administration were entrusted to a set of Colleges (kollegiia, boards), each with its own well-defined function and competency, such as army, navy, foreign affairs, treasury, commerce, justice, mining and industry, and so forth. At first there were nine Colleges, but their number eventually reached fourteen. The Colleges replaced the Muscovite prikazy, of which only a few had been rather functional in nature, although there was no formal act abrogating them, and some even survived Peter's reign (for instance, the Siberian prikaz). The

---

[1] Nor do we really know what happened to the professional clerks (diaki) of the Muscovite prikazy. Did they provide the backbone of the new institutions too?

[2] This was also the justification for Peter's law of imperial succession, although its rationale clearly conflicted with the notion of institutionalized impersonal government.

Colleges were supposedly set up on the Swedish model, on the principle of collegial responsibility rather than monocratic authority. As a matter of fact, practically all central administrative institutions in Europe at the time—even in France—operated on the collegial system, for they were the successors of the councils and boards of late feudal times. Peter, however, added his own rationale—namely, that several heads are better than one in thinking up solutions and in understanding problems. Moreover—and it was the decisive point— collegial responsibility, he felt, made for mutual surveillance by the members of the College; no single member would be in a position to pursue bad policies consistently or to acquire exclusive power. These were important considerations, indeed, to a ruler who was jealous of his own prestige and fully aware of the numerous failings of his assistants.

In 1711, on the eve of his departure for the ill-fated Pruth campaign, Peter appointed several of his closer collaborators to "mind the shop" in his absence, to take care of and decide all current affairs in his stead. This was the origin of the Senate. The institution, as well as its composition, underwent several changes in the course of Peter's reign, a sign that the emperor himself was as yet not quite certain of its basic function and definitive form. In the final analysis, the Senate emerged in 1721 as the highest coordinating and supervisory institution of the government, and it also had an ill-defined role in policy planning as well. The supervisory function of the Senate was given prominence with the appointment of a procurator-general of the Senate. At first, the procurator-general was an officer of the Guards who merely had to see to it that the senators did their job efficiently and honestly. Eventually, however, he was put in charge of the chancery of the Senate; he had to gather data and check on the local bureaus, plan the Senate's agenda, and act as liaison officer to and for the monarch. At the end of the reign, the Senate had become an organ of the regular administration: Presidents of the Colleges (at first of all, later only of the first three— army, navy, and foreign affairs) were ex-officio members; the emperor's closest favorites and personal companions, however, were not. Presumably, the elaboration of basic and long-range policy and the taking of extraordinary decisions, the essential functions of sovereign power, were to remain an exclusive prerogative of the ruler assisted by his immediate entourage. From the very beginning of the imperial regime, therefore, and not unnaturally so, the essential functions of planning and coordinating policy, of resolving jurisdictional conflicts between Colleges, were not given a regular institutional form, but remained at the discretion of the sovereign on an ad hoc basis. This worked reasonably well as long as the ruler was a man of the stature, personal drive, ability, and capacity for work of Peter the Great. But what would happen with an average individual at the helm of the state?

Inadequacy of planning, supervision, control, and honesty—these were the major problems that plagued Peter and his successors. Peter tried to cope with at least some of them by establishing two institutions: the *fiskaly*, headed by a *general-fiskal* subordinated to the procurator-general of the Senate, and the Preobrazhensky *prikaz* (note the use of the old term!) headed by the trusted, loyal, and ruthless Prince F. Iu. Romodanovsky. The *fiskaly*, as their name implies, were the guardians of the financial honesty of officials and bureaus. Dispatched to the provinces on a more or less regular basis, they checked accounts, reviewed files, gathered information on officials, and received denunciations or complaints of graft, bribery, and corruption. But who in turn was to check on the *fiskaly*? They were not above reproach either, the more so since they operated on a commission basis. They did not survive Peter's reign.

[margin note: fiskaly]

The Preobrazhensky *prikaz* was, in fact, the office of the political police. Its task was to seek out and repress disloyalty, treason, revolts, slander against members of the imperial family, any expression of discontent—whether word or deed. The *prikaz* acted primarily on the basis of denunciations—the dreaded *"slovo i delo gosudarevo"* ("word and deed relating to the monarch"), which in fact had been on the books since the Code of Alexis in 1649—and made itself feared by the brutality of its methods of investigation (triple torture of both denunciator and denounced) and the harshness of the punishments it meted out. The dread and hatred in which the names of Preobrazhensky *prikaz* and of Romodanovsky were held made it politic to abolish the institution ostentatiously in 1729. But obviously the empire could not do without a police, especially a preventive political police which, by the nature of its task, had to work in secrecy. Institutions similar to the Preobrazhensky *prikaz* remained permanent fixtures of the imperial government under varying and more or less innocuous names.[3] Under Alexander I, the political police was merged with the office of policemaster-general, also the head of the regular police of the capital. Eventually, the functions and methods of the political police of the eighteenth century (without physical torture) devolved on the Third Section of His Imperial Majesty's Own Chancery and the Corps of Gendarmes under Nicholas I.

[margin note: prikaz political police → to Ivan Grozni's oprechniki similarities]

Peter I had fashioned a comprehensive and orderly central administration which served as framework for the imperial government for most of its history. This was not the case, however, for local

[3] The secret police offices were as follows: Kantseliariia tainykh rozysknykh del, 1731; Tainaia ekspeditsiia pri Senate, 1763; Special chancery, 1810; Ministry of the Interior, 1819; Third Section, 1826.

government. Obviously, Peter had no clear or firm notion of what to do with respect to local affairs. Foreign models and theories were even less suited for imitation in the provinces than had been the case with the imperial institutions. As a result, Peter experimented a great deal, and still did not succeed in devising an effective and lasting framework. By something of a return to traditional ways, his successors managed to postpone a thorough reform until the Pugachev revolt forced Catherine II to do the job. There is no need in a survey such as this one to follow the vagaries of Peter's efforts with respect to local administration; a few words on the general trend and its outcome will suffice.

First, the empire was subdivided into eight provinces (*guberniia*), which by 1719 were eleven in number, to replace the numerous and varied divisions of the Tsardom of Muscovy. For a time each province was administered by the commander and officers of the regiment(s) quartered in it, but eventually this experiment was abandoned in favor of a return to a hierarchy of governors and *voevodas* (in cities and districts), appointed by the central government for short terms (two to four years as a rule). These officials combined judicial, administrative, fiscal, and police functions; they were assisted by a very small number of subordinate officials and clerks. The pattern of their subordination to the institutions on the national level was far from clear. In principle, of course, they were dependent upon the emperor, with whom the governors usually had the right to communicate directly. For practical purposes, however, they were subordinated to the Senate, or—during the latter's eclipse —to the Supreme Privy Council and the Cabinet of Ministers. Naturally, they also received instructions from, and had to render account to, some of the Colleges; but this aspect was not clearly defined. Last, but most important of all, the number and quality of these local officials left much to be desired. More frequently than not they were officers who were no longer fit for active duty in the military establishment because of age or wounds or sickness. At times, too, incompetent or disgraced officials from the central government were "exiled" to local administration. In short, they were second-string officials, not very familiar with civil and local affairs, ignorant of local conditions, and unable to become acquainted with them since they did not stay long at any one post. Inadequately and irregularly remunerated, they often had to fall back on the old *kormlenie* (feeding) system of Muscovite times, that is, they lived off the land from graft and contributions levied on the local population. Inefficient and corrupt, they were of more harm than benefit to either the local population or the central government.

It is true that Peter had toyed with the idea of putting local gov-

ernment into the hands of officials elected or selected from among
the local nobility. But this experiment did not work as planned, and
it was quickly abandoned. One of the main reasons for its failure
was the fact that compulsory state service prevented the nobility
from residing on their estates in the provinces. Nor did the Russian
nobility have the strong tradition of corporate organization on the
local level of the nobility of the Baltic provinces and Sweden, whose
system of local officials Peter had tried to imitate. But the notion was
not forgotten, and it became possible to implement it when a greater
number of nobles moved to the countryside.

[With respect to municipal administration, too, Peter wanted to
break radically with the past and introduce institutions that could
become the mainstay of municipal self-government and corporate
autonomy. He did not succeed, and the old reality was merely clad
in a new garb, for Russian circumstances proved wholly unadaptable
to the basic premises of the Western model. Peter organized the
urban merchants and tradesmen along the lines of Western corporations. To the merchant guilds and the corporations of the *posad*
(town) population, he gave a great degree of self-government, especially in judicial matters, through a system of *ratushas* (derived from
the German *Rathaus*), which in the large centers were headed by a
magistrat, and subordinated to the *general'nyi magistrat* in St.
Petersburg. But two factors proved insuperable stumbling blocks to
the success of this scheme: the Russian towns had no secure, conscious and well-organized class that could become the nucleus of
a patriciate and a strong bourgeoisie. There had been, it is true, a
number of prominent and rich merchants in Muscovy who had, on
occasion, displayed a sense of corporate identity. Of these, many
had died, and most of those remaining were Old Believers. This put
them at a legal disadvantage, and they were unwilling to participate
in the institutions of a state they rejected on religious principles. As
for the overwhelming majority of the urban population, it was a
hodgepodge of peasants on leave from villages and estates, petty
shopkeepers and artisans without cohesion or a tradition of self-
government.

The second factor in the abortion of the Petrine municipal institutions was failure to give them autonomy, initiative, and full
jurisdiction in all urban concerns, rights that were the very raison
d'être of municipal corporations in the West. In traditional Muscovite fashion, the municipal institutions were turned into instruments
of the towns' fiscal and service obligations to the state. In short,
their task was only to organize the collection of taxes and dues and
to be held responsible for the proper performance of government
service obligations on the part of their fellow citizens. The rich

unsuccessful break w/ past w/ re: administration

shunned the burdens and duties of municipal office, for they were not only extremely time-consuming, but fraught with great danger of economic ruin: the elected member of the *ratusha* or *magistrat* could not attend to his business, was at the mercy of the central authorities (or the governor), and in addition was held accountable with all his property for any failure or shortages in the collection of taxes and dues from the population. The essential features of the system were preserved after Peter's death, but the *magistraty* were subordinated to the *voevoda*. The abolition of the *general'nyi magistrat* (1728) only served to put the urban institutions under more direct and closer supervision of the Senate and the Colleges of the Treasury and of Justice. All these changes took place to the detriment of self-government and corporate autonomy; in this domain, too, we have to wait until Catherine II for a new departure.

A few words will suffice here on Peter's reform of the government of the Church. Patriarch Adrian having died in 1700, the tsar decided not to replace him. The office was filled on an interim basis by the "Caretaker of the Patriarch's See," Stefan Iavorsky. Although he had been appointed because he was considered to be favorable to Peter's policies, Iavorsky eventually turned on the emperor and denounced what he believed to be his ungodly, unchristian, and destructive ways. Peter resolved to put the Church under firm secular control. In 1721, after Iavorsky's death, the administration of the Church was entrusted to a collegial body, the Holy Synod, consisting of a number of clergymen appointed for a term (archbishops, bishops, abbots, and priests); the latter were mostly specialists in canon law, theology, or ecclesiastical administration. The emperor was the head of the Church, and he was represented in the synod by a lay official, the *ober-prokurator* (formally not a member of the synod, which consisted only of clergy). The functions of this lay official were similar to those of the procurator-general in the Senate: he had to see to it that the members of the synod worked in orderly and loyal fashion; he headed the synod chancery; and he served as a channel of communication between the synod and the sovereign. Naturally, this was potentially a position of great power that could, for all practical purposes, make a layman the virtual head of the ecclesiastical administration. This is what happened when the office was filled by strong, energetic, able men; for example, Prince Ia. P. Shakhovskoy in the eighteenth century and the notorious K. P. Pobedonostsev in the second half of the nineteenth.

The death of the Tsar Reformer (*tsar' preobrazovatel'*) and the insignificance of his successors pushed the problems relating to policy planning, coordination, and supervision into the forefront of official concern. We have seen how Prince A. D. Menshikov tried to fill the first emperor's shoes but was checked by other dignitaries and favorites who helped to bring about the formation of a new organ of government, the Supreme Privy Council. In a sense, this council was the successor of both the Senate (which continued to exist as an institution of routine administrative supervision without policy-making power) and the informal group of Peter's own collaborators and friends. It was its oligarchic aspect that brought about the council's downfall when Prince D. Golitsyn attempted to institutionalize on a permanent basis its power and privileged political position. Yet, the need remained for an institution that would devise, coordinate, and supervise general imperial policy on a regular basis. Anna's German favorites and their toadies were not able to perform this task adequately; nor did the Senate regain a leading position in her reign, since it was staffed with mediocre men and overshadowed by the favorites. Eventually, in 1731, a solution was found in a Cabinet of Ministers consisting of three members: A. Osterman, A. M. Cherkassky, and G. Golovkin, replaced on his death first by P. Iaguzhinsky, and then by A. P. Volynsky. The crafty and experienced Osterman determined foreign policy; the very energetic, ruthless, and able Volynsky tried to give a national and constructive direction to Anna's domestic policies; while Cherkassky appears to have been a good bureaucratic workhorse. As Anna was neither energetic nor able, the cabinet might have become a powerful institution, a new Supreme Privy Council and a challenge to the authority of Biron and his acolytes. This is what brought about the downfall and execution of Volynsky almost on the eve of Anna's death. With her passing and with the overthrow of Ivan VI, his mother the regent, and Marshal Münnich, the cabinet was abolished.

Elizabeth, who had acceded to the throne as a successor to and follower of the policies of her father, restored the Senate to a position of preeminence. It again became the highest institution of government, with wide powers of supervision, control, and coordination. But the senators were not suited to acting in concert as an effective policy-making and planning body; they were experienced dignitaries, but steeped in routine, and as individuals not very close to the sovereign. Empress Elizabeth's own laziness and lack of interest in government affairs again led to the rise of individual favorites who took over this vital function. Fortunately, Elizabeth found in the brothers Peter and Alexander Shuvalov individuals who were up to the task, whatever their personal morality and honesty. But rule by favorites is not an adequate answer to the essential need for planning and supervising state policy on an imperial scale. Favorites are too much concerned with their own prestige and material advantage; they also are terribly insecure, as they are dependent on the whims of a ruler who could turn away from them because of intrigues or a sudden change of mood.[4] The problem became most pressing when Elizabeth's government started to prepare for what turned out to be the Seven Years' War, a war that had to be fought against a powerful and able enemy, Frederick II of Prussia, in alliance with England. The original conception of the Petrine Senate and of Anna's Cabinet was revived: a "Special Conference at the Imperial Court" was set up to deal with the planning and prosecution of the war in its diplomatic as well as military aspect. Naturally, the conference became involved in routine matters, as they were connected with the supplying and recruiting of the army and the administration of occupied territories. Thus, at the time of the death of Elizabeth, the Special Conference had turned into a genuine crown council.

In the first chapter we mentioned the emergence of an elite group of officials whose powers and functions, centered on the Senate, had become routinized by the end of Elizabeth's reign. Together with the Special Conference, this elite appeared to constitute a ruling circle with a stable membership that would provide continuity and *esprit de suite* to the policies of the state. But Russia was still an autocracy; it was the very existence and strength of the autocracy that made possible the formation of such a political elite and the routinization of its influence without arousing the rank-and-file nobility. On the death of Elizabeth the preservation of this pattern depended on the good will of her successor and on the situation at court. But Peter III, either on his own or at the suggestion of his favorites (his Holstein relatives, and a few German generals), decided to rule with his own men. He abolished the Special Conference, replaced the procurator-general of the Senate, and eventually pushed the Senate into the background. In their stead he surrounded himself with men who came to form a special council (it had no official name) in which D. V. Volkov, as the emperor's privy secretary, played the decisive role in domestic affairs, while the Holstein princes and generals dominated the military and diplomatic fields. It seemed a return to the conditions that had prevailed at the time of the Supreme Privy Council under Menshikov or the *Bironovshchina*.

As if to confirm the worst suspicions, Peter III let General Baron Korf, his crony and newly appointed policemaster-general of St. Petersburg, organize a far-flung police network independent of control by the Senate and local governors. These measures not only jeopardized the constructive institutional work of the senators under Elizabeth, but also threatened the elite, as well as the hopes and security of the rank-and-file nobles, who found themselves cut off

[4] They are also involved in and vulnerable to intrigues by court factions.

from access to the sovereign and at the mercy of the police. The decline in power and loss of authority of the Senate was the symbol of this development. Little wonder that the senators eagerly joined the rank-and-file nobility (as represented by the Guards regiments) in the coup that overthrew Peter III. No sooner had Catherine II ascended the throne than she restored the Senate to its previous position.

On her accession Catherine II clearly indicated her intention to govern with the assistance of the regular elite. This, however, did not solve the question of policy coordination and planning, which had been the major practical problem since Peter the Great and which entailed a normal pattern of channels of communication between the monarch and the most important government institutions, in the capital as well as in the provinces. Looking to the West, and drawing on the experience with the original Senate, the Cabinet of Anna, and the Special Conference of the preceding reign, the highest officials found it more desirable to give permanent institutional form to the body of the monarch's trusted advisors. This was the notion behind the proposal put forward by N. I. Panin in 1762; a regular and permanent imperial council, a kind of cabinet, should be set up to assist the ruler and assume the responsibility of coordinating, planning, and supervising basic policy decisions. At first, Catherine seemed to favor the plan; but members of her entourage argued that the council would serve as the entering wedge to a restriction of her autocratic power (Panin's closeness to Grand Duke Paul, whose tutor he was, made it easy to put the worst interpretation on his designs). This reaction was probably natural on the part of those who feared exclusion from the sovereign's inner circle. Catherine's most active supporters, the Orlovs, no doubt speaking for the Guards, expressed a similar sentiment, fearing that with the creation of a council, they would be deprived of free access to the sovereign's favors. In any event, Catherine II did not act on Panin's proposal, and let the matter lapse for the duration of her reign. Energetic and able as she was, she herself could—and did—give direction and *esprit de suite* to policy, and effectively coordinate all aspects of government. In this latter task she was ably assisted by Prince A. Viazemsky who, as procurator-general of the Senate throughout practically the entire reign, acted as her principal agent and chief minister, and kept the machinery of administration well oiled and going. Under his procuratorship, the Senate ceased to be an important advisory body, but its area of competence as the highest administrative and judiciary institution of the empire was enlarged and consolidated. Of all Catherine's many lovers and personal favorites, only G. A. Potemkin played a significant political role, and that was mainly in imperial matters, as we have seen. But he exercised his power only through Catherine, so that his influence never threatened the monarch's absolute and final authority.

Under the whiplash of the Pugachev rebellion, Catherine turned her attention to local government and produced a set of reforms that served as framework for public life in the provinces until the introduction of the *zemstvos* in 1864. By the statute of 1775 the territory of the empire was divided into forty provinces *(guberniia)*[5] of about the same population (300,000 to 400,000) and roughly comparable areas. The arrangement was a bit mechanical—the boundaries disregarded economic or historic units—but it had the advantage of clarity and relative simplicity. Each *guberniia* was headed by a governor; the more important ones (or several lesser ones combined) were put under a governor-general or a vicegerent *(namestnik)*. The governor or governor-general was the personal representative of the monarch, and as such he had direct access to the sovereign. His main function was to supervise and coordinate the various organs of local administration, without (at least in theory) directly interfering with their routine operation. On the *guberniia* or lower levels, too, the offices of local administration were set up along functional lines, with a major effort being made to separate the judiciary from the administration. But as the governor retained authority to control and supervise the housekeeping side of the judiciary, the latter was far from independent. Each of the local functional offices was subordinated to its respective College; ultimate supervision and coordination was the function of the Senate. All these reforms followed the basic orientation set by Peter I.

But Catherine II also innovated.[6] She involved the upper classes of the population—the nobility and the members of the first two merchant guilds in the cities—in direct participation in local administration. The nobility of each *guberniia,* organized into a corporation, elected its marshal, and on the district *(uezd)* level, also a constable *(zemskii ispravnik)*. The latter policed his territory, imposed punishment for minor offenses, punished recalcitrant serfs (at the request of the landlord), pursued criminals, and saw to the proper performance of various public works (such as maintenance of roads and riverways). The marshal of the nobility (there was also a district marshal, as well as a provincial one) was the spokesman for the needs and

---

[5] Their number varied subsequently. In 1796 there were 51 *gubernii,* reflecting the empire's territorial expansion.

[6] Some of Catherine's solutions were discussed earlier (see Chapter 1). She also seems to have responded to suggestions made by officials (e.g., Prince Ia. Shakhovskoy in 1762) and by the requests contained in the instructions for the deputies to the Commission of 1767.

guardian of the interests of his class. He also appointed guardians for noble orphans and mediated or arbitrated disputes involving inheritances and property, if both parties requested him to do so. He kept the roster of the local nobility and inscribed new members upon proper certification of their letters patent or other credentials. Finally, all institutions of a charitable character, primarily those for the nobility, were under the marshal's trusteeship. Limited as it was, this active participation in local affairs was a great step forward in the history of the post-Petrine nobility. It signified—and helped to foster—the development of a local, corporate life in the *guberniia* not so much in administrative matters, as in cultural and social life.

In fact, the *portée* of the nobility's participation in local government was quite restricted. In the first place, the autocratic traditions and the practices of bureaucratic guidance and control did not disappear. The governor remained too dominant a figure to permit the marshal of the nobility to develop into a genuine autonomous focus of power. There were a few rare exceptions to this, of course; for example, in those cases when the marshal himself was a prominent personage who had retired to live on his estate without severing all his connections at court. The marshal, and *a fortiori* the constable, in the final analysis, turned out to be little more than assistants to the bureaucracy and executors of instructions received from above. In case of conflict between governor and marshal, the authorities in St. Petersburg, and the monarch, almost invariably sided with the former. In the second place, the manpower available to fill the elected offices was far from first-rate. The best-educated, ambitious, and ablest nobles entered state service; bent upon a successful career, they did not care to serve merely as local elected officials, a service that gave neither promotion in the Table of Ranks nor much social consideration, and only a small salary.[7] This was why the elected officials were usually second-rate, stick-in-the-mud types, or former officers and bureaucrats who had retired with a modest rank. The former were obviously no match for the bureaucracy and fulfilled their duty as representatives of their electors rather sloppily; the latter brought to their new role the habits of obedience and submissiveness acquired in their previous service. Neither proved adequate defenders of and powerful spokesmen for the interests of their constituents. The poverty of the elected officials left them open to corruption and financial pressure on the part of the

---

[7] It is characteristic that elected functions were called "service by election" ("*sluzhba po vyboram*"). Under Alexander I elected officials were rewarded with promotion in rank after a very long period of service and repeated reelection. But the best men were usually attracted by the central authorities and wound up in the bureaucracy.

wealthy, the governor, and his aides. Yet, despite these serious limitations, the provincial reform of Catherine II did mark a turning point in Russian history, for it encouraged the formation of a genuine "society" (obshchestvo) in the provinces as well as in the capitals.

The arrangement for the towns paralleled that for the provinces. It suffered from the same weaknesses—even more so, since the elected municipal officials had no authority over a most significant part of the town's population: the nobles who owned and lived in townhouses. It is fair to say, however, that the reform, complemented by the Charter to the Towns of 1785, did eliminate some of the more onerous obligations and legal limitations that lay on the urban citizenry. It set the stage and created the conditions for the urban development that took place in the first half of the nineteenth century under the stimulus of economic expansion.

The reign of Paul I did not witness any significant changes in the direction the political development of the empire had taken under his mother's rule. Paul relied more on his entourage (whose composition changed frequently) and gave free rein to his own capriciousness and ill temper. Thus, for example, the effectiveness of the Senate as the chief administrative institution was severely strained by the frequent changes of procurator-generals. But we notice an increasingly powerful trend to give up the collegial principle and the emergence of the monocratic system of ministerial responsibility. The trend received its full legislative implementation in the reign of Paul's successor.[8]

The assassination of Paul was greeted, as we have noted, with great joy by the elite in the capital, who had lived in fear of his caprices and who were determined to prevent the recurrence of such a tyrannical regime. The younger generation of the educated elite was well prepared and articulate; its members had the ear of the new emperor, Alexander I. But before this group could make its influence felt, another segment of society seized the initiative to bring about political reform.

In a way that was reminiscent of the pattern in the coup against Peter III, Paul had been dethroned by men with close ties to Catherine's ruling elite, the group of dignitaries (and their families and clients) who, since the reign of Elizabeth, had exercised the greatest influence on the monarch and in the state. These men feared intrusion and takeover by new men, the favorites of the emperor (for example, Kutaisov, Arakcheev). Their deed done, the conspirators,

---

[8] It should also be mentioned that Paul I regularized the order of succession by issuing the Statute of the Imperial Family, 1797. The statute, however, did not prevent confusion in 1825.

led by the energetic and able Count von der Pahlen, attempted to bind the young Alexander to a policy that in large measure would have implemented the plans of D. Golitsyn and N. I. Panin for a restricted and powerful crown council.[9] In short, they wanted Alexander to institutionalize on a permanent basis the elite's right to a decisive role in government. But Alexander outmaneuvered the conspirators; for as they could not dethrone him, they had little hold on him. The young monarch also took full advantage of his personal charisma, a charisma inherent in the autocratic nature of political sovereignty in Russia. The conspirators needed Alexander to bring about the change they hoped for. It was the paradox of all would-be reformers: they had to expect the limitations of autocracy from the autocratic power itself.

Two other groups from within the elite of Russian society helped Alexander to free himself from his father's murderers. The leaders of the Senate came to his assistance by putting forth suggestions on strengthening the government and securing the rule of law. They proposed to achieve these goals by virtually giving the Senate the rights of registration and remonstrance.[10] Some suggestions went further by proposing to enlarge the membership of the Senate and endow it with a representative character by having each province send one nobleman-delegate, either elected or appointed from a list of local nominees. A narrowly based permanent crown council was not to the liking of the senators, and it was their support that allowed Alexander to resist the pressure of von der Pahlen and even exile him to his estates within a few months of his accession.

At the same time, while the "senatorial party" was putting forth its plans, Alexander gathered a small group of his own old friends who became, for a while, his closest advisors. The so-called Unofficial Committee formed by these friends consisted of A. Czartoryski, V. Kochubei, N. N. Novosil'tsev, and P. Stroganov, and it was assisted from behind the scenes by the emperor's former tutor, F. C. La Harpe. This group of men of Alexander's own generation represented another facet of the political attitudes prevalent among the ruling elite in the second half of the eighteenth century: it was, one might say, a more liberal and modern version of enlightened despotism. They aimed at implementing the basic ideas of Catherine's Nakaz

[9] It may not be amiss to note the fact that N. P. Panin was the nephew of N. I. Panin, author of the project for a council in 1762. The Baltic background of von der Pahlen may also have had something to do with his political orientation.

[10] Reference is to the right exercised by the French *parlements*, especially the one in Paris, during the Ancien Régime, of registering (or refusing to do so) the edicts and laws issued by the king. The *parlements* also had the privilege of remonstrating with the king if they believed his acts to be contrary to the traditions and constitution of the French monarchy.

by means of an orderly, rationalistic, bureaucratic administration and the benevolent exercise of the monarch's autocratic power. In this respect, the members of the Unofficial Committee were the bureaucratic counterpart of the cultural elite that was making its voice heard in the journals and books of the period. Characteristically for this generation, they took a technocratic approach to government: they insisted that all reforms and changes be the work of a small committee of experts who would labor in secret; the plans issuing from this committee were to be implemented at once, through the autocratic fiat of the ruler. Whether the Unofficial Committee's suggestions, had they been carried out fully in all their implications, would have led to a "constitutional" regime is a hypothetical and therefore unanswerable question.

Having parried von der Pahlen's threat to his authority, Alexander proceeded to reward both his allies to some degree. In 1802 the Senate was given what seemed to be an implied privilege of remonstrance. At the same time, at the suggestion of the Unofficial Committee, ministries were established to replace the inefficient and outdated Colleges. The new institutions were given a monocratic pattern of organization and thus satisfied the demand for more rationality and hierarchical subordination in the bureaucracy. As might have been expected, the Senate's attempt to remonstrate was nipped in the bud the next year. The Senate thereafter became an almost exclusively judiciary body, the highest institution of appeal (besides the emperor, of course) for both criminal and civil cases.

Alexander relied on the bureaucratic approach and the ministries to introduce a number of structural reforms into the administration —reforms which, however, neither diminished the monarch's autocratic power nor affected the social composition of the empire. The bureaucratic, rationalistic reform of the government went into high gear when M. M. Speransky became Alexander's close collaborator about 1806. The organization of the ministries that had been established in 1802 was now completed. It followed the military pattern of a staff command: The minister was the commander-in-chief, and his subordinates were staff officers and directors of technical sections. The relationship between the ministries and the provincial administration was clearly defined in functional terms: the individual bureaus of local government were subordinated to the relevant ministries, and only the governor was allowed to communicate with both the Senate and the emperor. On January 1, 1810, Alexander I solemnly inaugurated the Council of State. Originally it had been designed to act as a policy-planning body and as the final legislative drafting committee under the emperor. As it turned out, however, it never became a policy-planning organ, but it did serve to review all final drafts of new legislation. Its three sections (codification, economy, military), moreover, also played an important role in gathering and digesting pertinent data and in working out comprehensive regulations for each of these areas of national life.

In 1809 Speransky presented a comprehensive plan of reform, in which the Council of State was but the top level of a whole structure. He proposed the creation of a pyramid of consultative assemblies, *dumas*, on the local, provincial, and national levels. The scheme was interpreted, especially by its critics, as a grand constitutional design that aimed at abrogating the autocracy and at replacing it with a representative constitutional monarchy. Of course, we do not know how the plan would have worked out had it been put into operation, but it is unlikely that it would have led to genuine constitutionalism. Probably, however, it would have initiated a gradual but far-reaching social transformation. By beginning a slow and conservative emancipation of the serfs and thus freeing the individual, it would have laid the foundations of a *bürgerliche Gesellschaft*. Internal opposition, as well as the French invasion, precluded the plan's ever being put into effect. Because the Senate was relegated to a judiciary function and the Council of State did not fill the role assigned to it in Speransky's plan, there was still no body for coordinating the actions of the various ministers. The Committee of Ministers, which grew out of a need for mutual consultation among several ministers on problems crossing their respective jurisdictions, could easily have taken over the responsibility of coordinating and planning policy for the empire. But ever-watchful, determined not to have his autocratic power reduced by even one whit, Alexander did not allow this to happen. The Committee of Ministers received only consultative authority on an ad hoc basis; its meetings were never attended by all the ministers at once, and it had no way of making all the ministers follow the same policy. Each minister discussed his information and policy, and received his instructions, at the weekly private meetings the emperor held separately with him. To supervise and, on occasion, coordinate the execution of his orders, Alexander relied on the corps of his own *fliugel'* and *general ad'iutanty*. They became his *missi dominici* and special instruments in the investigation or solution of any unexpected and unusual problem. This system gave the Russian government a more militaristic character than it had ever had in the eighteenth century.

In the area of local government, Alexander's reign brought no changes significant enough to be noted here. But it is interesting that in the first quarter of the nineteenth century serious discussions took place as to the desirability of organizing Russian local government along federal lines. As a result of a growing awareness of the multinational character of the empire (which we have seen reflected in the Siberian statute of 1822 concerning the natives) and of its centrifugal forces, a proposal was made to give the larger component parts more autonomy, even some degree of self-government, and to guarantee their traditional culture and customs. No doubt such proposals reflected the new arrangements provided for Poland and Finland. One such federal scheme for the empire was proposed by N. N. Novosil'tsev, the governor-general of the former Lithuanian provinces, in his Charter Plan of 1820. More limited in scope, and strictly bureaucratic in character, was the system of governor-generalships combining several *gubernii* advocated by the Minister of the Interior, A. D. Balashov, and tried out in the governor-generalship created out of the provinces of Tambov, Orel, Voronezh, Tula, and Riazan', of which he became the head. Here too, the aim was to deconcentrate the overly centralized, and consequently cumbersome, machinery of administration that could not move without a direct command from St. Petersburg. But all these schemes went so much against the tradition of the autocracy and the grain of bureaucratic practice that they did not come to fruition, and they were never revived.

In the first quarter of the nineteenth century there were also significant efforts at creating more professionalized and better-trained cadres of officials. It was quite evident that mere length of service and good connections were not adequate qualifications for a corps of officials that had to cope with increasingly complex and challenging problems. More finesse, tact, education, and knowledge were required of officials, since in some areas of administration, the bureaucracy had to cooperate with "society," as well as promote and protect individual initiative and enterprise, particularly in the realms of economy and culture. The better education of the nobility, the more numerous opportunities for training, were laying the groundwork for a better—more responsible and more responsive—corps of officials. Paul I had reintroduced the *iunker* corps for "on-the-job" training in the Senate; Alexander I founded the Juridical Institute, whose primary task, as its name indicates, was to train government personnel. The *lycée* at Tsarskoe Selo founded in 1811 was conceived as the training school for future high officials, especially in the diplomatic corps; its curriculum provided for a well-rounded general education stressing political economy and jurisprudence, while the teachers and the director emphasized the elite character of the students and their special civic and social responsibilities.

Of course, the universities and such special institutions as Bezborodko's *lycée* in Nezhin (for general education), the Demidov *lycée* in Iaroslavl' (for jurisprudence), and the *lycée* of Odessa (general education) trained an ever-growing number of students, many of whom still joined government service upon graduation. As a result of these developments, the relative role of ecclesiastical schools in providing members of the bureaucracy declined, although until the middle of the nineteenth century, graduates of these institutions constituted a respectable proportion (about 20 percent) of civil officials, especially on the local level. The modernization of the curricula of ecclesiastical schools (carried through in 1808) explains the persistence of their role in the training of bureaucrats, though in the long run the reform's most important contribution was to make possible the formation of a solid contingent of scholars, academics, and scientists.

Keenly aware of the need for educated government servants, Speransky persuaded Alexander I to decree the minimum level of educational achievement required for promotion beyond the first group of lower ranks in the Table of Ranks (up to the ninth), and to provide for a set of examinations to check on the candidates' knowledge. So great was the outcry from the bureaucrats and the rank-and-file nobility that Alexander retreated; after the fall of Speransky (1812), the legislation was allowed to lapse. Still, the point had been made, and thereafter a relatively high level of knowledge and achievement was expected for the higher positions and ranks, examination or no examination. All this paved the way for the emergence of a new type of Russian official: the well-educated, well-prepared nobleman who could perform specialized technical tasks with competence, and who, imbued with a high ideal of responsibility toward the nation, made of this service an exclusive lifelong career. He was the backbone of the devoted bureaucracy that eventually helped draft and carry through the reforms of the 1860s.

Unfortunately, with respect to the lower levels of the bureaucracy, no such hopeful development and improvement can be detected in our period. The clerks continued to be recruited somewhat haphazardly among *raznochintsy*, children of soldiers and of *meshchane*. Too poor to obtain secondary education, they learned the routine of office procedure during a more or less long apprenticeship. Because they had no expectation of rising above their lowly position, outside the Table of Ranks, they had no ambition to better themselves. They were frightened of any change in routine that could threaten their position. Woefully underpaid, they were open to graft, bribery, and corruption. In the final analysis, they constituted one of the greatest stumbling blocks in carrying out the reforms and changes devised by far-seeing and liberal dignitaries and educated high officials.[11]

---

[11] They are the most numerous of the bureaucratic types who populate the novels of social criticism in the nineteenth century, from Gogol to Saltykov-Shchedrin.

Another barrier to effective administration, especially in the area of justice, needs to be mentioned briefly: the absence of an up-to-date and easily available code, or compilation of laws. The last formal code dated back to 1649 (the so-called Sobornoe ulozhenie of Tsar Alexis). Since then, the amount of new legislation had been staggering in its quantity and in its innovative character. It had never been collected or systematized, and much of it was unavailable even to those who needed to refer to it. Similar cases were frequently decided in different ways on the basis of contradictory legislation, or ad hoc decisions, depending on which was available to the judge at the time. There was a crying need for a systematic compilation and codification of the government's decrees. In the course of the eighteenth century, ten commissions had made a start on the task, but none had come even near completion. Speransky took over the job in 1809 from the commission set up in 1802 (in which Radishchev played an important role, but which had not completed the assignment either). He first thought of saving time by elaborating a skeleton code of legal principles, on the basis of foreign models. His fall prevented the completion of the scheme, which was no loss, for the procedure he wanted to follow did not take sufficiently into account the historical traditions and peculiarities of the Russian legal development. His successor, Baron Rennenkampf, was correct in believing that the first task of codification consisted in finding out and collecting the legal tradition of Russia. He started to do it, but did not finish the task. Eventually, after 1825, Speransky was assigned the job of codification again; this time he tackled it from the correct end, that is, first collecting the existing laws, then sorting out those still in force in preparation for a new code. The work was completed between 1828 and 1835.

The Economy

In any discussion of a country's economic development, it is first necessary to have a clear notion of the state of its basic resource—that is, the population. In the case of Russia during the period covered in this book, the picture is .clear: continuous and dramatic growth. The first census of the taxable male population taken in 1719 counted 7,788,927 souls, including members of the regular army. The seventh census in 1815 yielded the figure of 21,538,207 souls of the same categories.[1] The territorial expansion accounted for only a small fraction of this increase, since the most extensive conquests, in the south and southeast, were quite empty of population. We should keep this fact of dramatic population increase in mind, for it helps to account for the state's growing resources, in spite of the low level of the economy, as we shall see.

Peter I had not only aimed at bringing Russia closer to Western Europe, but also at developing the nation's resources to provide support for a powerful military establishment and an active diplomacy. The long and difficult war against Sweden, as we have seen, also served to draw Peter's attention to economic needs and policies. As had been the case with his administrative and military reforms, Peter was strongly influenced by the prevailing practices and theories of the West. In the economic domain these were primarily associated with mercantile conceptions and policies, to which was added a touch of German *Kameralismus*, as exemplified in Prussia. Peter's receptivity to mercantilism was furthered by the Muscovite tradition of state control and monopoly of important sectors of the economy (foreign trade, Siberian furs). Because the prime needs were military, and under conditions of a shortage of private capital, the state was

---

[1] The increase continued after 1815. In 1815 there were 23,845,328; in 1850, 28,555,360. In the territory covered by the first census, the increase had been from 6,345,101 (1719) to 13,353,247 (1815).

naturally led to play a major role in directing and financing economic development.

Peter's was what we call today a "crash program": the creation of an industrial and commercial base for a modern (by early eighteenth-century standards) big power in short time, while fighting a war, with very few traditions and skills available among the population. The results were impressive on paper, but economists still debate the extent to which the accomplishment was economically sound and lasting. There is no doubt that his policy put the country under great pressure and imposed a heavy burden on its population. But was this burden a crippling one, as maintained by Miliukov over half a century ago, or merely very heavy, though absorbed in the long run, as claimed more recently by Kafengauz? Was successful economic development limited to Peter's reign or did it continue after the emperor's death? These are some of the questions that economists have not yet answered, for there is no agreement on the indicators to be used in calculating the costs and achievements of the policy.[2] At this point, the historian can record only disagreement.

It has been mentioned earlier that Peter changed the unit of direct taxation from the household to the individual male. This tactic not only raised the total amount of monies collected, but made escape from taxation obviously more difficult for the individual peasant. It resulted in the massive flight of peasants to the open steppe in the east and south and to the forests, beyond the reach of the government's agents.[3] But capitation was not the only means available to the state for obtaining revenue. Increasingly popular with Russian officials in the eighteenth century—in imitation of Western practices—were indirect taxes on consumer goods and state regalias and monopolies. Naturally, these indirect taxes lay most heavily on the lower classes, since they increased the price of such essential commodities as salt and alcohol.[4] Finally, the turnover of goods within the empire was made into a source of additional revenue, even though it hampered the development of a stable internal pattern of exchange.

The fiscal burden did not grow lighter after the end of the Great Northern War and the death of Peter I. During the government by

[2] Quite clearly, political events of the twentieth century influence these judgments.
[3] The figure for the capitation tax is meaningless unless we know earning and purchasing powers. It is a calculation that Professor A. Gerschenkron has undertaken, but he has not yet published his results. There is also a great deal of dispute as to the numbers involved in peasant flights and in interpreting the evidence from which these can be derived.
[4] Indirect taxes rose by 242 percent, while direct taxes increased by 146 percent between 1724 and 1769 (per taxable person).

the Supreme Privy Council, there was something of a tax relief, but it took the form of the government giving up the collection of arrears. The inability of the government to lower the taxes was due to the fact that its expenditures not only kept up, but rose constantly. While the relative peace that prevailed after the death of Peter did lead to a decline in the share of military expenditures, it was more than compensated for by a rise in the share of administrative and court expenses.[5] In the final analysis, the modernization of the country, and particularly its diplomatic and military role as a large European power, the elegance and wealth of the court, the cost of administration and the parasitism of favorites—all combined to make for a twofold rise in state expenditures in over half a century.[6] Under Catherine II expenditures increased still more dramatically, as a result of her expansionist policies and her active involvement in European diplomatic and military crises over Poland and the French Revolution. It is true that part of the increased fiscal burden was absorbed by the population growth we noted at the beginning of the chapter,[7] but the very high level of taxation doubtless prevented the accumulation of resources (capital) that could have been invested more productively.

In the field of industrial development, Peter is often credited with having established and developed most of Russia's extracting and processing industries. With some qualifications, for example, the not-insignificant domestic production of artillery in the sixteenth and seventeenth centuries, this is correct. To fill military and naval needs, Peter expanded the existing facilities and created new ones, mainly in the new capital, St. Petersburg. These factories, shipyards, and manufactures belonged to the state and were administered by government bureaus; their technical and managerial personnel were selected from among regular state servants, usually from the military, while the labor force was forcibly recruited from among state peasants and convicts. Peter also promoted industrial expansion by private entrepreneurs. The state was lavish in granting subsidies, preferential tariffs, bounties, and temporary monopoly privileges. But there was little capital available in the population at large, and the merchant class—the traditional source of entrepreneurs and capital in the West—had neither the tradition nor the means and skills to contribute significantly. Hope was therefore pinned on the nobility;

[5] In 1725, of the total expenditures, 6,541,000 rubles (64.5 percent) went for the military establishment, and 3,600,000 for the administration. In 1767, the respective figures were 9,648,000 (47.6 percent) for military, and 10,623,000 for the administration.

[6] From 10,141,000 rubles in 1725 to 20,271,000 in 1767.

[7] In 1719 the male taxable population was 5,570,000, while in 1762 it had risen to 7,362,000.

Peter encouraged, nay pressured, his closest aides, high dignitaries, and courtiers to undertake industrial and mining operations. He provided them with state capital for a start and guaranteed steady returns. But most important of all, and this is what indirectly explains why the merchant class was not drawn more into the process, he made it possible to obtain labor. The bulk of the labor force had to be drawn from the peasantry, and since the peasantry was no longer free, the transfer of labor from agriculture to industry and mining took place by government decree or the decision of individual serf owners. Peter made it possible to have entire villages "ascribed" to factories or mines, under a system which required the serfs (ascribed peasants) to work in these enterprises, sometimes located at a considerable distance from the village, during the months they were not occupied with field work. Another way to provide labor was to give (or sell) serfs directly to factories or mines—the so-called *possession-nye krest'iane*, under which they were transformed into industrial bond labor, that is to say, industrial serfs. The fate of the peasants transferred to industry and mining was horrible: They had to perform work to which they were not accustomed, under conditions that were comparable to those of penal labor.

Historians have usually stressed that many of the enterprises founded under Peter were economically not sound (silk weaving, production of various luxury items), or that excessive government regulation precluded their "natural" development. It is true that most of these creations did not outlive Peter, or else proved so much of a loss that they were abandoned even earlier. It is also quite true that the "aristocracy" in Peter's entourage were not genuinely committed to their industrial enterprises and failed to develop the managerial or business skills necessary for their success. By the end of the 1720s most of the original noble entrepreneurs had withdrawn from the field. But it is not correct to assert that Peter's entire program of industrialization—whatever its initial cost and economic efficiency—failed to survive his reign. The basic industries he had helped to develop, if not actually to establish, remained active and continued to grow, even if not at as rapid or economically rational a pace as modern economists might wish. This was the case with the mining and smelting enterprises of the Urals, the shipbuilding and production of essential military and naval equipment in St. Petersburg, the Baltic ports, and Archangel. In these areas we also note more participation by merchants and "middle class" people, a situation that caused the conflict between them and the nobility over their right to buy villages and serfs for transfer or ascription to their industrial enterprises.

In the middle of the eighteenth century there occurred a distinct pick-up in industrial and commercial activity. The policy of Peter

Shuvalov under Elizabeth, by abolishing most of the internal customs barriers, resulted in a liberalization and quickening of the
country's economic life. The policy culminated in Peter III's decree
making it easy for peasants to bring their produce to the local town
market by abolishing passport and registration requirements at city
gates. These measures contributed in a significant way to drawing
the peasantry more and more into a trade and market economy. As
has been shown, the major entrepreneurs from among the peasantry
and lower urban classes in the early nineteenth century trace their
origins and economic success to this liberalization of domestic trade,
reinforced by the expansion of urban population and consumption.
The Shuvalovs also reduced the government's direct management
and ownership of industry by transferring many state enterprises to
private hands. In so doing, they hoped to involve the richer nobility
in more active participation in the economy. The results did not
always justify these hopes, for quite a few state enterprises had to
be bought back by the government at great loss to the treasury and
to the enterprise itself. But in many instances, particularly the Ural
foundries and the textile manufactures around Moscow, the noble
proprietor sold out to a merchant or an entrepreneur from the lower
classes (including even serfs; for example, the textiles at Ivanovo
Voznesensk). In this way impetus was given to the development of
an entrepreneurial middle class and renewed expansion of the industrial potential of the empire. The trend continued under Catherine II
and bore its most remarkable fruits in the second quarter of the
nineteenth century.

Against these successes there should be put, however, a general
decline of the mines and foundries in the Urals, a decline that set
in in the 1760s and was hastened by the Pugachev rebellion. The
traditional explanation is that serf labor proved too expensive and
inefficient. Another factor was that the availability of serf labor
eliminated any incentive to introduce labor-saving machinery which
would not only increase production, but also improve quality. But
for the future of the Urals, the most fateful factor was the prohibi-
tive cost of transportation. Waterways were the cheapest means, but
they were unreliable, besides being unusable part of the year. All
other facilities were extremely expensive, for they required large
investments in manpower and cattle (horses). This fact should be
constantly borne in mind when dealing with Russia's relative back-
wardness and the slow pace of its "modernization." Transportation
facilities also played a major role in limiting the areas receptive to
modern trade and industry to those that were close to good waterways; this accounted for the rapid development of an export-
oriented agriculture in the south.

The dominant economic factor in imperial Russia throughout our period was serfdom. It determined all facets of economic as well as social relationships. A detailed economic analysis of serfdom is beyond the scope of this study, and of the competence of the author as well. Moreover, much work on the microeconomic level needs still to be done before we can say with assurance what the economic characteristics and effects of the system were, how viable it was, how beneficial to the owners, how much of a handicap for the entire economy. Naturally, the problem is closely related to the nature and state of Russian agriculture not only because serfdom concerned primarily agrarian organization, but also because Russia was an overwhelmingly rural country.

It is well to remember, first of all, that the units of agricultural exploitation were extremely small. The traditional custom of inheritance among land and serf owners was to divide the patrimony equally, in terms of the quality of each share, as well as the quantity. A middling-sized estate might be splintered into, say, six to eight tiny estates within two or three generations. In addition, none of these small estates was in one piece; each contained a more or less equal amount of all the types of land and resources of the original property. Splintering of estates made intensive agriculture very difficult, since one could not efficiently improve very small parcels. Furthermore, an owner's possessions, more frequently than not, were scattered among several estates over a large area, each cluster of serf households or villages being separated from the other by as many as several hundred miles; at times, they were at opposite ends of European Russia. If a village commune constituted a living social unit—though its members might belong to several owners—its pattern of activity was usually dominated by the requirements of the three-field system. In view of the strip and splinter condition of the holdings, the three-field system tied the peasants to a rigid, traditional schedule of field work. For even one member of the community to depart from the schedule might upset a very delicate balance, create havoc, and at harvest time bring disaster. This situation was a further cause for hampering initiative, extra investment, and meliorative measures, either on the part of the peasants themselves or that of their masters. It also explains the stubborn resistance to any change in the traditional routine ways, even when the landlord furnished the new equipment or showed the way.

Of course, at the bottom of this traditionalism and stubborn rigidity was the fact of an extremely low productivity that reduced agriculture to a permanently hazardous and marginal operation. For this state of affairs there were first natural causes—the rigorous climate and a very short growing period, so that a crop could easily suffer from bad weather. The soil, especially in the central regions, was frequently poor, or had been exhausted. Only the newly opened southern steppes put into cultivation on a large scale at the very end of the eighteenth and the beginning of the nineteenth centuries enjoyed good harvests. The Russian peasant was poor in cattle because of limited pastures and ignorance of the fodder crops that were revolutionizing Europe at the time and providing an alternate to grain; he therefore had little manure to restore fertility to an exhausted soil. In the newly settled lands of the eastern regions beyond the Volga, the wasteful slash and burn technique was applied to forest lands, and similarly wasteful methods were used in the newly plowed steppes. All this explains why the yields were extremely low in Russia, even compared with contemporary France (not to speak of England, which was in the forefront of agricultural improvement in the eighteenth century). A yield of 3 to 1 seeded was considered average, and a yield of 4 to 5 times the seed was good indeed; in *ancien régime* France, it was the latter that was considered average. The marginal character of the yields obviously meant that one bad year was enough to create want, and a succession of two or three poor harvests meant starvation. Naturally, there was little surplus available for the market, even had the latter been more accessible to the average peasant.

In short, the peasant was fortunate if he produced enough for his and his family's survival; he had little hope of improving his lot by much, and this explains his passivity and fatalism. To pay the capitation, as well as the other taxes and dues, and to purchase the few items he could not produce himself, the peasant frequently resorted to such subsidiary activities as cartage, working as a laborer in the towns in the winter, and craft and cottage industries. Rare was the peasant (whether private or state serf) who by dint of lucky accident —such as success in a small carrying trade, cartage revenue, or craft work—managed to make a little surplus. But how could he invest it? The surplus, like the peasant himself, was at the mercy of the landlord, and it was difficult to find good use for it within the communal pattern. The peasant's outlook, therefore, remained distribution- and subsistence-oriented, as is typical of a premodern agrarian society whose members give prime consideration to survival and preservation of the traditional pattern and system of values, and for whom the maximization of benefits and productivity for their own sake are meaningless.

To this picture there must be added the attitudes of the nobility, the land- and serf-owning class, whose decisions directly affected the life of the peasants under their control. We have mentioned the splintering of estates that made for inefficient units of exploitation. In addition, there was a great deal of confusion about boundaries between estates. The complicated pattern of inheritance made for frequent disputes among heirs; the long-felt absence of a general, reliable land survey (it was started only in 1765 and proceeded quite slowly) compounded this insecurity. Spoliation and raids on neighboring lands by richer, better-connected and arrogant landlords was a frequent occurrence, compounded by the inadequacy and weakness of the local administration. Finally, like their peasants, the large majority of the nobility was quite poor by contemporary European standards. It has been calculated that a minimum of one hundred "souls" (that is, male serfs) was needed to permit a way of life that included an adequate education and a reasonable service career. But in 1777 only 17 percent of noble households possessed this many serfs. As a result, the bulk of the nobility stayed in government service, so as to have the opportunity to live in the cities and in the hope of special rewards for good performance. Obviously, the nobleman in service could not devote much attention to his estates or supervise his peasants. He left the management to bailiffs or hired managers (not infrequently foreigners in the second half of the eighteenth century), who took care of their own interests rather than those of the landlord.

The nobility's way of life and focus on state service perpetuated an attitude that was indifferent and unreceptive to the concept of maximization of profits for its own sake. This is not to say that the landlords were not interested in higher incomes, but they were not able or concerned enough to take the necessary, but difficult, steps to secure them on a long-term basis: reorganize their estates; introduce modern accounting methods, techniques, and machinery; invest capital (which was short, to be sure, but since the reign of Peter III there had been banks for the nobility that granted loans on advantageous terms).[8] Only the very, very wealthy were able to think in such terms, or the rare individual who had been bitten by the bug of modernization and Europeanization.

All this had as its consequence—paradoxical as it may seem at first glance—to make most noble estate owners not so much producers as purchasers of grain. Although the exact figures have not been determined (there were wide fluctuations regionally and chronologically), there is no mistaking the trend of rising grain prices throughout the eighteenth century. Higher prices were no doubt the consequence of the devaluation of the currency (about 13 percent between 1725 and 1767, and it dropped some more after Catherine started issuing paper assignats), of the heavy burden of indirect

[8] Most of the loans made were small in amount and for consumption purposes only.

taxation, and of the high cost of transportation, as well as the growing demand of towns and cities. In the last quarter of the eighteenth century, the export of grain abroad resulted in a still greater demand and rise in prices. For the landlord, this trend had two opposite consequences: On the one hand, it became more expensive for him to live in town, with many domestics, and to support—as he had to —his own serfs in case of famine. On the other hand, the higher prices of grain gave him an incentive to increase the productivity of his lands. This led the noble landowner to a re-evaluation of the methods of managing his estate and of securing an income from his serfs' labor.

Basically, there were two types of obligations serfs had toward their master: Under one kind of system, their main function was to work their lord's land—this was the corvée (barshchina)—and only the time not taken up by the lord's work could be spent by them for their own benefit. Under the second kind of system, the serfs paid the lord a yearly fixed amount—in cash or in kind, or, most frequently, a combination of the two—the so-called quitrent (obrok); they were then at liberty to spend their time as they saw fit (exception being made for service obligations imposed by the state, such as road maintenance). Naturally, the serfs enjoyed greater freedom and wider scope in organizing their activities under the quitrent system; it allowed them to leave the village for long periods to seek work elsewhere, provided that they paid their quitrent. The quitrent in cash was relatively moderate and, most important of all, quite stable (although because cash incomes were low, it was often not easy for the serfs to raise even these sums). From the landlord's point of view, the quitrent yielded a relatively predictable but not very large income; an income, however, that declined in the course of our period, as the purchasing power of the currency dropped and prices rose.

By the 1760s landlords felt they were in a bad squeeze: grain prices and the cost of living were rising, while revenues remained stable or declined relative to purchasing power. They believed the solution to their plight lay in greater availability of grain, either to lower purchase prices or to provide a greater marketable surplus for a bigger profit. More important, they attributed their plight to the peasants' leaving the land to work in the cities and bringing about a decline in agricultural production. This was not so, but the reasoning of the landlords proved to have serious implications. They believed that one way of increasing income was to force the peasants to stay in the countryside and to till the soil in preference to any other occupation. We therefore have here not what the Soviets call the intensification of feudal exploitation, but rather what Professor

Confino has so aptly termed a renaissance of the corvée system as the major way of exploiting serf labor. On many estates, the peasants were put back on the corvée, or on a mixed system of quitrent and corvée obligations. From the point of view of the serfs, especially for those who had been on a lax quitrent for a long time, this meant the reimposition of the most oppressive conditions. The landlord who wished to maximize the productivity of his estate (either directly or through his manager) saw to it that the corvée was in fact performed fully; he also increased the amount of land to be worked by the serfs, and thus forced the peasants to devote practically all their energies to working for the lord, retaining only Sundays and holidays (and not always even these) to cultivate their own plots.[9]

Resentment was naturally high among the peasantry. Furthermore, the corvée system was not very efficient, and it did not encourage improvements in techniques and equipment, so that the productivity of Russian agriculture did not rise (except for the new territories in the south). In the final analysis, while the renaissance of the corvée system resulted in the large-scale, but wasteful exploitation of the new lands in the Ukraine and the export of Russian grain abroad, it did not bring about an improvement in the central and eastern provinces. On the contrary, it stymied innovation and tied many peasants to unproductive lands, creating regional overpopulation and agrarian pauperization. Thus the corvée offensive cured the plight of neither serf nor marginal landlord in the central provinces; it was, rather, a significant factor in the slow economic development of the empire, and in what has been called the crisis of the serf system in the second quarter of the nineteenth century.

However, it should also be said that in the late eighteenth and early nineteenth centuries there is some evidence of a progressive economic outlook on the part of members of the educated elites. Under the impact of Western ideas and examples, especially physiocracy, there developed greater concern for and interest in the betterment of agriculture. Catherine II founded the Free Imperial Economic Society, 1765, for the purpose of improvement of agriculture, experimentation with new techniques and crops, surveying of resources, and collecting of information that could be usefully disseminated among landlords. Admittedly, the Free Economic Society and its work found a favorable response among the average nobility only very slowly: in its first decades, the society attracted the attention of but a very few progressive nobles, most of whom were associated

---

[9] This was what prompted Paul's decree on three days of corvée a week as legal maximum. Sunday had to be kept free of all work. The decree proved almost unenforceable.

with the court and hoped to make themselves favorably known to the empress. The suggestions and propaganda generated by the society on behalf of better tools and methods did not have the desired effect, since most nobles lacked the capital or understanding to put the advice into practice. All things considered, however, the society created a climate of opinion and accumulated a store of information and experience that proved of great value by the middle of the nineteenth century. Interestingly enough, Catherine permitted the first public discussion of the economic value of serfdom under the auspices of the Free Economic Society. Prizes were offered for the best essays in response to such questions as: Is it more advantageous to have the serf own his land or only his movables? Which is economically more profitable, serf or free labor? The competitions stimulated thinking about the character and future of serfdom, Russia's "peculiar institution"—thinking that bore fruit in the first quarter of the nineteenth century in preparation for eventual emancipation.

Although of course there was trade—the products of craft industries were marketed, sometimes at great distances—commerce was still in a rather primitive state. One of the characteristic features of Russian trade was that much of it was carried on at fairs. Its greatest handicap was lack of capital, and more particularly of credit. Russia had no banking system, even of the limited type that had become a mainstay of continental Europe's economy. Curiously enough, as in medieval times in the West, credit was most likely to be available within the framework of closed communities or societies. Hence the role of those Old Believer communities whose members' property reverted to the community at their death, and whose scattered network of affiliates made possible the use of letters of credit, promissory notes, and even verbal instructions. Little wonder that the Old Believers formed a substantial element in the merchant class and that they eventually became major entrepreneurs, prominent in the development of light consumer industries (textiles, leather, sugar).

Most towns developed with difficulty and slowly, with the exception of St. Petersburg and the new creations in the south (Odessa, Nikolaev). The major reason was that until 1785 (and even thereafter, to some extent) the towns were organized primarily to perform government services. They were local markets and centers of production only for a limited number of goods that were used by the inhabitants or bought by peasants from nearby villages. The towns' fiscal obligations put an excessive burden on the urban population and handicapped their economic initiative. It should also be mentioned that much of the goods consumed or used by the nobles living

in the towns—and they were the richest and greatest consumers—
was produced by their own serfs. Many of the latter, it is true,
became highly skilled craftsmen and artists, producing magnificent
luxury objects, but they remained serfs, legally not part of the urban
population. Moreover, these artisan activities did not contribute to a
market economy, for only in rare cases did the nobleman allow his
serf craftsmen and artists to produce work for sale.)

In the domain of economic development, too, the first decades of
the nineteenth century are marked by the emergence of new trends,
ideas, patterns. Most significant was the reception of the new economic notions associated with the school of Adam Smith by Russia's
governing and intellectual elites. It made for the acceptance of a
larger role for private initiative, for the favoring of economic enterprise for its own sake, for the feeling that the pursuit of economic
gain is not morally reprehensible, but in fact will benefit not only
entrepreneurs, but also society at large. Under Russian conditions,
it was believed, this orientation toward individual free enterprise
might have to be qualified: there was not enough know-how and
capital, so that the government would have to provide encouragement and aid. It was the government that first helped to popularize
the new ideas by publishing translations of Adam Smith's works in
official periodicals, by permitting wide-ranging discussion of his
ideas, and by introducing courses and chairs of political economy
in the newly opened educational institutions (universities, lycées).
The opinions and writings, as well as the administrative policy, of
such dignitaries as M. M. Speransky and Admiral N. S. Mordvinov
contributed to freeing the government from its traditional practices
of mercantilist and paternalistic controls in favor of greater freedom of enterprise and more liberal international trade policies.[10]
Finally, the government also sponsored trade schools and training
centers in an effort at acquainting a larger number of Russians with
new modes of production and commerce. As had been the case a century earlier, the necessities of war also helped to create new demands,
present new challenges, and discourage dependence on the outside world. There is little doubt that much entrepreneurial talent and
capital came to light in the process of supplying the Russian armies
and of participating in the rebuilding of areas devastated by war,
especially Moscow and other cities in Napoleon's path.[11]

These stirrings, however, were handicapped under Alexander I

[10] For example, the so-called free tariff of 1809 and the relaxation of duties after
1815.
[11] The sons of those peasants who had begun to trade actively after the relaxation of passport requirements in 1762 were frequently in a position to supply the
armies. Their earnings in this activity allowed them to participate actively in the
rebuilding of Moscow.

not only by war, but also by the excessively heavy fiscal burden that
the struggle against France imposed. The printing of paper money
(assignats) started by Catherine II was continued and reached huge
proportions, so that the value of Russia's currency kept falling. Thus,
in 1805 one paper ruble was worth 73 silver kopecks, while in 1814
it was worth only 20. The fiscal instability and the growing deficit,
only partly covered by English subsidies, prevented the development
of an efficient and stable credit system. This situation lasted to the
end of the reign, and only in the next reign, as a result of Count
Kankrin's cautious policy of fiscal stabilization, were the conditions
created for a more rapid economic takeoff. In the meantime, too, the
pattern of Russia's international trade had undergone change. At the
beginning of the eighteenth century, the empire had been primarily
an importer of manufactured goods (mainly from England), and .only
a modest exporter of a few items like naval stores, lumber, and furs.
At the end of the eighteenth and in the early nineteenth centuries,
the situation was quite different: not only had the total amount of
international trade risen very sharply, but its character had changed
too. Russia was still a heavy importer, but not of luxury consumer
goods only; manufactured goods, especially industrial machinery,
were occupying an increasingly prominent place in imports. Still
more significant was the fact that England had turned away from
Russia as its main supplier of naval stores, while Russia's major
staple for export had become grain. Significant as this change was,
its full impact was not felt until much later, beyond the period of
our concern here; yet it was heralding Russia's participation in the
economic exchanges of an industrialized capitalist world *in statu
nascendi.*

Social Classes

In this chapter we shall limit ourselves to a consideration of the Great Russian population only, as we have dealt with non-Russian natives and Cossacks in the chapter on the empire. It is difficult to separate a discussion of social classes from that of political and economic developments, and we have therefore dealt with some aspects of Russian society in earlier contexts; they should be kept in mind when reading what follows.

The first class of the empire was, naturally, the nobility, although it was quite small numerically (between ½ and 1 percent of the total population).[1] It may not be totally out of place to mention a few basic features of the Russian nobility before the reign of Peter the Great to set the framework for the subsequent history of this class. Noble status in Muscovy was not connected with the possession of a particular landed estate, formerly a fief, as in the case, say, of France. Nobility was a matter of birth and service (rod i chin). This meant that, in principle, accession to noble status was normally through service, although progess was slow, and it usually required a few generations to reach the highest rank of boiar, for instance. Conversely, a noble family declined to the status of commoner if its members did not serve, or served in low offices. The combination of service and birth was the determining factor in defining a nobleman's position within the service class.

There were complicated and numerous gradations within the nobility—from the boiars, who formed the tsar's court and were entrusted with major military and administrative assignments, through the

---

[1] On comparable territory, the number of noblemen increased as follows: 1744–1745, 37,326 (0.504 percent of total population); 1762–1763, 49,777 (0.590 percent); 1795, 77,199 (0.680 percent). For the total empire, the figure was 193,132 in 1795 (1.032 percent), 224,626 in 1815 (1.080 percent), 362,546 in 1833 (1.391 percent). Clearly, the increase was not only a natural one, but shows that the class remained open to newcomers throughout our period. I owe these figures to the kindness of Professor A. Kahan of the University of Chicago.

ranks of Moscow "courtiers" (*dvoriane, that is, service men*), to the lower echelons of "boiars' children," town service men (that is, those attached to garrison towns), ending with the lowest categories (*pantsyrnye boiare, odnodvortsy*) whose members guarded the "open field" frontier of the realm and gradually shaded off into the free peasantry. Success in service by one member raised the status of his relatives; if in the next generation service was performed on the same level, the entire family (*rod*) would be elevated. Thereafter, it did not behoove a member of such a family to accept assignments of lower standing, or to serve under the command of someone whose family was less distinguished; this was the *mestnichestvo* system. The system had two undesirable consequences: First, it hindered the tsar's freedom in appointing the best-qualified person to a post. Conversely, it made it difficult to raise one's family to higher status through merit and performance of duty, or through the tsar's personal favor. These two consequences combined to bring about a limitation to the practice of *mestnichestvo* during the seventeenth century (for example, at the start of every campaign the tsar decreed that military appointments were not to be subject to *mestnichestvo* considerations). It was eventually abolished in 1682, yet it is worthy of note in order to point out the tension between birth and service that constituted an important element in the nobility's condition from the seventeenth century on.

Bent upon transforming the old patterns and modernizing the country, Peter the Great needed servitors who not only would do his bidding, but also actively and voluntarily assist him in this pursuit. He would not bother with the services of those who were unwilling and unqualified, merely because their birth or status entitled them to positions of eminence. He therefore relied almost entirely on performance in service in recruiting his advisors and assistants. It was only to be expected that members of prominent families would be at an advantage, if they were willing to accept Peter's policies wholeheartedly. After all, they had better education, training, and experience, as well as the connections to make themselves known to the ruler. Such was the case of Marshal B. Sheremetev or, in the civilian domain, of Princes F. Romodanovsky and D. Golitsyn. Though Peter did not radically change the composition of the nobility, especially of its upper stratum, he did base it squarely on service. Naturally, he also admitted to the ranks of the government elite a large number of men from the lower ranks of state servants, or from junior and impoverished branches of old families who in the past would have had little chance of rising high, for example, the Golovkins, A. Tolstoy, I. Nepliuev. He freely recruited and generously promoted foreigners and even commoners; among the latter, A. D.

Menshikov is the best known, though hardly a typical, example. Thereafter, birth gave only the normal advantage of better opportunities, but it was rank in service that determined an individual's status; a rank, moreover, that could not be transmitted to children. It is true that noble titles—prince and the new ones of count and baron introduced by Peter—were hereditary. But they did not confer genuine status advantages, since according to Russian custom all sons inherited the title, creating a plethora of titled but impoverished and insignificant individuals (for example, the character of Prince Myshkin in the *Idiot*). After Peter's time, it was service rank and not hereditary title that conferred status in imperial Russia.

Peter's practice received its legal and definitive form with the promulgation of the Table of Ranks in 1721. It established fourteen ranks (the first being the highest), in three parallel groups depending on the type of service—military, civil, and court. The names were taken from the German and more or less russified. In addition, the table stipulated that everyone should start service at the bottom of the ladder and receive promotion only for merit, extraordinary achievement, or length of service. Finally, nobility was closely related to rank, that is, a commoner who by virtue of his service reached the eighth rank (that of commissioned officer) would automatically receive hereditary nobility. In the nineteenth century the requirement was raised to the fifth rank, that is, staff officer; and Nicholas I abolished automatic ennoblement through the Table of Ranks altogether.

If we recall what has been said about the Muscovite nobility, we shall readily see that, in its basic conception, the Table of Ranks was not revolutionary, even though its formal aspects were quite novel. This explains why the table met with no opposition and only a little grumbling. The members of the old upper families of Muscovy who were loyally serving Peter received high ranks automatically; as for the rank-and-file state servants, they welcomed the table as a convenient instrument for their own rise to higher status (in the absence of institutions for secular education, there was no serious threat of competition from commoners). It is therefore not very remarkable that the nobility rapidly internalized the Table of Ranks' basic conception as the foundation and framework of their way of life and outlook. The important thing for the nobles was to obtain a respectable rank, or to make sure that their children received the opportunity of easily attaining such a rank. The social aspirations of the nobility were therefore going to be focused on two points: to facilitate for their children the first steps in climbing the table's rungs, and to prevent commoners from taking too great an advantage of the provision for automatic ennoblement.

What was new in the table was that it implied compulsory, *permanent*, lifelong service. Opposition to permanent service largely stemmed from the fact that it prevented the nobleman from returning regularly to his estate to oversee its management and take care of his private interests. Objection to the requirement that the service career begin at the lowest rank (common soldier or sailor) was to be expected from members of a privileged class who considered it demeaning to serve with peasants and other commoners and be subjected along with them to degrading punishments. An interesting turn was given to this problem by the fact that, in a modernizing and rationally oriented state, success in service depended on formal skills which were best acquired through education. The service nobility therefore demanded that their children have an opportunity to receive an education that would allow them to bypass the apprenticeship period as soldiers, sailors, or clerks.

The first overt expression of this attitude took place, as we have seen, in 1730, in connection with the Supreme Privy Council's attempt at imposing some limitations on Anna. It is rather significant that the demands for exemption from service as soldiers or sailors, and for a special school for noble children to prepare for officer rank, should have been put forward by the rank-and-file service nobility (although some were of distinguished birth). The second demand was easily met with the establishment of the Corps of Cadets in 1731. Such a school had been advocated still earlier by dignitaries as necessary for the better training of officers; significantly, too, its original statute was drawn up by Marshal Münnich, who served as the Corps' first director, on the model of the contemporary German and Austrian *Ritterakademien*. Another request had been put forward by the nobility in 1730, that compulsory service be limited to thirty or twenty-five years. Anna did not grant the request right away, and only in 1734 did it become possible to retire after thirty years of service. This was not much of a concession, since after thirty years a candidate for retirement was hardly of much use anyway; and no one who had a successful career would want to retire, as this was the time when he could expect to obtain the highest rewards in prestige and material benefits for his long and loyal exertions. In the course of the reign of Elizabeth, however, there was a further relaxation of service obligations, so that at the end of her life, a nobleman could retire after twenty years of service. As we have seen, it was Peter III who finally gave the nobles permission not to serve altogether, although his famous Manifesto of February 18, 1762, still reserved preferential treatment and status to those who served. At any rate, the manifesto reiterated the expectation that the nobility would give their children an education appropriate to their class and service status.

The latter point shows that the terms of the discussion concerning the rights and status of the nobility had shifted between the promulgation of the Table of Ranks and the accession of Catherine II. Let us consider the question primarily on the basis of the instructions given to the deputies, and of the debates to which they gave rise, at the Legislative Commission of 1767. The crux of the debate was whether the nobility should remain an open class or its ranks be considered closed. In other words, whether the provisions of the Table of Ranks should continue to be applied to the letter. The spokesmen for the conservatives were prepared to ratify the *fait accompli* and did not intend to try to reverse the role played by the table since Peter's time; but they insisted that in the future nobility be granted only by imperial letters patent and that the practice of automatic ennoblement, as a consequence of promotion in the field or by decree of some dignitary, cease completely. Those who argued for keeping open access to the nobility were not commoners, but petty service men from the border areas. To them, the Table of Ranks offered the only opportunity of rising in the social hierarchy through their own efforts. The discussion ended inconclusively. The provisions of the Table of Ranks were never abrogated; commoners and petty servitors could enter the nobility by dint of service, and rank remained the basic factor in one's status—witness even such an "aristocratic" young man as Prince Kurakin, who felt that as long as he remained in a low rank, he could not show himself in good society.

The discussion in the Legislative Commission of 1767, however, had brought to the fore a basic criterion of nobility that literally was not stated in the Table of Ranks. The defenders of a closed nobility argued that nobility was a matter of moral sense and education. The former could be acquired only in a noble milieu (ironically, Prince M. M. Shcherbatov, who made this argument, was to castigate the nobility for not providing such a milieu); the latter, of course, had to be secured through schooling. Leaving aside the obvious polemical and rhetorical aspects of the argument, it is quite true that education provided the principal means of access to rank and status. General education in its Westernizing form was the hallmark of the elite, whether noble or not. But for the nobility it was to be a *sine qua non*, as the manifesto of Peter III stressed. Education, indeed, enhanced the chances of a career. A minimum was actually a prerequisite; it helped to overcome such disabilities as low birth (for example, Troshchinsky, Speransky), poverty (Derzhavin, Arakcheev); it was also considered the precondition of genuine civilization, so that membership in the elite depended on education, not on birth or wealth. This is the reason for the nobility advocating in 1730 more opportunities for education and recognition (in terms of ranks and preferment) for having obtained it; the same argument was repeated in 1767. The nobles felt that having obtained education, they should be rewarded by ranks; this the government was perfectly willing to grant them, since it did not threaten its authority, nor preclude using the talents of educated nonnobles.

It proved more difficult for the state to satisfy the demand for more educational opportunities. The main reason was financial, but Russia also did not have the personnel and facilities necessary to fulfill this demand on a large scale. The nobility insisted on the state providing education because it did not have the means to do it itself —a fact that only served to stress once more the dependence of the first class of the realm on the state. The average members of the nobility had to enter state service as the only means for leading the Westernized way of life he craved and giving his children an adequate education. Catherine II, and even more so Alexander I, met the wishes of the nobility by opening new schools that prepared nobles for professional service careers in a variety of fields. One may view Alexander's founding of the *lycée* at Tsarskoe Selo as part of an effort to reserve for the nobility easy access to and monopoly of the upper rungs of service.

By the time of the accession of Catherine II, the state no longer depended on the service of all noblemen. The government had hardly any use for the poorly educated and unambitious stick-in-the-mud nobles. Subordinate positions could be, and were, filled by commoners and foreigners. On the other hand, it had become desirable to have the nobility play a more active role in the countryside, as leaders of economic and cultural progress and as keepers of law and order.[2] Besides, those nobles who were largely Westernized in their way of life and culture yearned for activities outside state service. The latter fitted in well with the new orientation that Catherine II wanted to give the Russian polity. Prompted by the administrative deficiencies that became manifest during the Pugachev rebellion, Catherine II gave the local nobility a share in provincial government. The trend found its legislative culmination in the Charter to the Nobility of 1785.

The charter established the Russian nobility for the first time as an estate of the realm, organizing it into provincial corporations. The act also gave a definition of the nobility, which in its ambiguity characterized the fluidity of that class: it included the moral criterion advocated by Shcherbatov, but its practical realization had

---

[2] The relatively greater effectiveness of individual serf owners in controlling the peasantry is illustrated by the fact that most runaway serfs in the Volga area in the first half of the eighteenth century were state peasants.

to take place within the framework of the Table of Ranks (qualified by imperial discretion). Membership in the various provincial corporations of the nobility, however, was defined more clearly: the local nobles, as a corporate body, had to admit new nobles to their ranks, making sure that the necessary documents or letters patent had been produced, and keep a roster of all members. It was at this time that a new roster of the nobility was compiled—the *rodoslovnaia kniga,* based on the seventeenth-century *barkhatnaia kniga*—which, interestingly enough, had separate sections for princely families, old Muscovite service nobility, and nobility acquired through service since Peter the Great, though in fact these distinctions were not meaningful.[3] As has been frequently pointed out, it is in periods of decline and doubt that historical justifications and reliance on old documents become particularly important, for they serve to defend privileges, not functions. The nobility was further distinguished by the right to trial by their peers and exemption from corporal punishment. In separate legislation Catherine II granted the nobles exemption from direct taxation and the exclusive right to own real estate, especially settled estates containing serfs. These last two privileges were abrogated by Alexander I. More significant, however, than these rights, which did not weigh very heavily with the whims of an autocrat as the reign of Paul I showed, or which could be circumvented without difficulty, as demonstrated by Nicholas I, was the fact that the nobility was recognized as an estate, and a privileged one at that; and that it was invited to participate in the local affairs of its province. It also was encouraged to strike out in other directions where it could display its leadership and justify its exalted status by furthering the progress of the country.

It is not easy to determine how these expectations fared in reality. Russian literature has left us the image of a provincial nobility that was boorish, cruel, poor, and uneducated. The assemblies of the provincial nobility that met periodically to elect marshals served a social, particularly matrimonial, rather than a political or cultural function. The empire's cultural, economic, and public life remained concentrated in the capitals. Yet, it is but fair to say that thanks to the charter, local life did indeed develop. Without becoming a permanent resident, the educated, intelligent, successful, and active nobleman did begin to visit his province more frequently, participating in the assemblies of the nobility. Knowing that he would find companionable neighbors, he stayed on his estate for lengthier

---

[3] We also have a rash of genealogies of individual families, largely based on fantasy and the desire to prove that their ancestor came to serve the Grand Duke of Moscow from a foreign country. B. Veselovsky has convincingly demolished the value of these genealogical works.

periods to rest or to restore his finances. In so doing, he introduced provincial society to a more sophisticated way of life—to books, theater, education, music, conversation. In short, provincial life did follow that of the capitals, although at a more leisurely pace, and without losing all its old-fashioned forms and traditions. The Charter of 1785 provided the framework of the nobleman's life in the provinces until 1864, and served as a necessary prerequisite for the organization of the zemstvo institutions at that date.

So far we have not given sufficient attention to one facet of the nobleman's existence that was a major and permanent feature of his way of life and that determined his outlook: besides everything else, and at times exclusively so, he was a serf owner (which meant also landowner, except in the few cases when a nobleman only owned a few domestic serfs). Serfdom provided him with the means he needed to perform state service and lead a "civilized" way of life. We have considered the economic side of serfdom and of the agriculture based on it. We need not return to it here, except to repeat that for the vast majority of the nobility, serf labor meant not wealth but only the minimum essential for their way of life, provided they used the produce of their estates for their own consumption.

It is difficult to generalize about the history of a significant social class over the span of a century and a half. The Russian nobility, too, presents a wide spectrum of conditions; in the absence of detailed concrete statistical information that would take into account contemporary values and patterns, it is impossible to subdivide it into meaningful and clear categories. The following remarks aim only at indicating a few salient features of the nobleman as a serf owner, without any claim to statistical or typological precision. It is well to remember that, in the overwhelming majority of cases, the nobleman did not directly interfere in the life of his serfs in the villages; he stayed aloof from the routine aspects of agricultural production—and understandably so, since he had to be away from his estate most of his life, on service. The majority of the serfs working the land were rarely in direct contact with their master, albeit they had to work for him and fear his retribution if their payments or labor services were not forthcoming on time. In most cases, the estate—rather its agricultural operations—was supervised by bailiffs (elected or appointed by the landlord) or managers hired for the purpose. The serfs, obviously, preferred to deal with the former, since he was one of them, while the manager frequently came with new ideas and methods, was keen on an immediate high profit, and aimed at "modernizing." It was the household serfs who were most exposed to the masters' whims, caprices, brutality, and lewdness. Their fate was indeed a sad one, for they were never sure of the next day, even though, as in the ante-bellum South, there may have been the compensation of participating in the greater comfort and plenty of the master's household. Serfdom, like slavery, was grim; it dehumanized the serf and brutalized the master. There is no need to repeat here all the horrors that Russian literature has chronicled so faithfully and with such intensity of human and moral feeling.

There is, however, one aspect that may be worth mentioning briefly, since it has not always received due attention. By the middle of the eighteenth century, the Russian nobleman had become Westernized, that is, he had not only adopted the garb, but also many of the comforts, objects of daily use and luxuries, notions of refinement, learning, music, and arts—in short the way of life—of the European upper classes of the time. His pattern of living did not yet constitute a civilization, but it had most of its external appurtenances. The civilization would come in the early nineteenth century when the Western European externals would be combined with genuinely Russian creative elements. In any event, the noble serf owner wanted to surround himself with those things that signified his belonging to Western civilized society. Although he did not reside on his estate permanently, he wanted to be able to do so in the manner to which he had grown accustomed while on service in the capitals. If he was rich enough to own or build a house in the city, he wanted it to be the proper environment for the Westernized style of life that was expected of him by his peers and superiors. Thus he tried to reenact in his townhouse, or on his estate, his ideal of the proper European style of life. This pattern spread widely in the second half of the eighteenth century and continued to do so in the early nineteenth. It was reinforced by the burning of Moscow in 1812. Indeed, the tragedy led to the destruction of many old mansions and townhouses; when new ones were built to replace them, they were built according to European fashions, with all the latest conveniences and luxuries. During the invasion, many nobles fled the old capital, and brought to the provinces, where they sought refuge, their conception of the proper style of life for the nobility. Their influence proved lasting among their neighbors.

In all this the serfs played an important role, albeit an involuntary and passive one. Their labor provided the means that allowed their masters to pursue the style of life to which they aspired. Most frequently, it resulted in heavier impositions, greater exactions and exploitation (including such terrible things as the sale of villages or individual peasants to raise cash). Serf artisans built and decorated the master's lodgings according to his new foreign tastes. Household serfs were frequently required to wear Western garb, serve at table according to French etiquette, and prepare the new exotic dishes that were ordered by the master and his guests. They had to be musicians, actors, and dancers, as well as grooms, coachmen, dog trainers, valets, and butlers. Against their will, driven on by the whip and other forms of abuse, the serfs were drawn into the new, Europeanized style of life of their lord. If the master was kind, they might even feel some pride in belonging to such a luxurious and "modern" household. Obviously, in most cases, this style of life meant only increased oppression and sorrow. Thus, the nobleman's European ways came to be identified with the worst features of serfdom; they confirmed the serfs in feeling that their master had turned into an alien, a man of another culture, an individual who seemed almost different in kind. These serf owners were the objects of most violent hatred and profound resentment. The serfs felt sold out to alien masters who had perverted the original character of bondage and subverted the traditional balance and social economy of a truly Christian society. When they revolted, they vented their resentment and fury on the new, Western things, as well as on their Westernized oppressors. Yet, in spite of themselves, and very gradually, something of these Western innovations was incorporated by the Russian peasants into their way of life, as is amply illustrated by Russian literature of the middle nineteenth century.

So far we have spoken of the peasantry as if it were a homogeneous class. This was far from being the case, and it is time that we also take notice of the variety within the peasant class. The peasants, of course, represented the overwhelming majority of the empire's population, about 95 percent. Until the publication of the Digest of Russian Laws (Svod zakonov, 1832), the peasantry was a congeries of the most varied and complicated groups, and only the codification introduced uniformity by creating an "estate of agriculturists" for juridical purposes. Most of the groups, however, even in the eighteenth century, contained quite a small number of people; they were only the "remnants of history," illustrating by their existence the multiple ways in which Russian society had gradually come into being over the centuries. In as short a survey as this one, it is impossible to deal adequately with any of these groups, and it is better to ignore them altogether. Obviously, non-Russian natives constituted, in most cases, special categories too.[4]

The great majority of the Russian peasantry exclusive of Cossacks fell into two groups: state peasants and private serfs. There were only a very few scattered free peasant groups left by 1767, and most

---

[4] The only sizable small category was that of *odnodvortsy*, that is, single homesteaders—the descendants of petty service men (yeomen) in the seventeenth century who had declined to the status of free peasants. Non-Russian agriculturists were usually included in the state peasant administration.

of these had disappeared by the end of the century. The two principal categories were roughly equal in number, with state peasants slightly more numerous in the middle of the eighteenth century, and the private serfs in turn slightly more numerous in the beginning of the nineteenth century. After secularization, the serfs belonging to monasteries and episcopal sees became state peasants. There were also peasants belonging to the emperor personally, or to members of the imperial family—the so-called appanage, udel'nye, peasants; in most respects, however, they were identified with state peasants and need not be considered separately.

The village communities of state peasants were administered and supervised by officials either specially appointed to villages and districts inhabited by such peasants, or members of the regular local administration. The peasants had to pay a fixed amount of capitation (podushnaia) and quitrent (obrok) to the state, as well as perform various services, such as maintenance of roads and bridges. (There was a special category of postal peasants who had to maintain horses, relay stations, and furnish drivers). They had an important part in organizing communal life in their own villages; and provided that they paid their taxes and performed the services regularly, they were left alone. Except for the prohibition on leaving without special authorization and passports, they were quite free to pursue their traditional ways and their daily routine. The only serious threat that hung over their heads was to be given away to private owners, or to be attached to a factory. As long as the rulers remained lavish in rewarding their courtiers and loyal servants with serfs— Elizabeth, Catherine II, Paul were extremely lavish—this was a source of great anxiety. The practice was discontinued in the reign of Alexander I. Thereafter, they had to cope only with inefficient and corrupt local officials, until Count Kiselev's reform (1842) gave them a better administration under a separate Ministry of State Domains.

After our sketch of the economic aspect of serfdom and of the nobles as serf owners, there remains little to be said about the private serfs. Let us repeat for emphasis that the material condition of the serf was extremely precarious because of the low yield of Russian agriculture, the heavy burden of dues and payments to both the state and the lord, and—most important of all—because he was at the mercy of his master's whims, especially if he was taken into the household as a domestic serf. In the second half of the eighteenth century, many landowners who returned or retired to their estates proceeded to supervise them more closely. They wanted to organize the serfs more efficiently and increase their productivity, sometimes by introducing new crops and techniques. But their notions of organization and efficiency were usually derived from the military model with which they had become acquainted while in service. Thus they applied to their estates some of the techniques of rationalization, bureaucratization, and modernization they had learned in the military. The more superficial and comical instances of such efforts included, for example, the requirement that serfs march in step to and from the fields, with trumpets sounding and drums beating; the firing of a gun to indicate the end of the work day; the organization of work gangs along military models. Military rules and regulations, "articles of war," served as the basis for punishment; voluminous codes of laws and rules that attempted—vainly—to regulate every detail of the peasant's routine. This kind of interference in village life served as a great irritant to the peasants, who were not willing to adapt to such foolishness. Brusque and sudden changes in traditional ways, new plans, experiments in improvement and modernization, as rapidly abandoned as they had been introduced, all produced an atmosphere of disorder and capriciousness. More serious, however, was the grave threat these whims of the lord offered to the normal pattern of cultivation which, as it was, produced only the bare minimum. And we have not yet mentioned the instances when serfs were called from the fields to lay out gardens, dig fountains, and work on the beautification of the lord's estate; all too frequently, even in the case of as careful, reasonable, and considerate a lord as the memoirist A. Bolotov, this work had to be performed at the height of harvest or planting time. In short, the serf's routine and relative security were always at the mercy of the lord's whim. This alone would have made serfdom hateful; but in addition, as we have shown, it was economically backward and burdensome.

From whatever side the peasant looked at it, serfdom, as it was in Russia in the middle of the eighteenth century, was plain wrong: it was wrong morally; it violated Muscovite tradition; it went against the peasant's sense of community and social justice. Indeed, seen in this perspective, the major cause for the evil of serfdom was that the noble serf owner had been interposed between the state and the people. In the traditional view, everybody served the tsar so as to enable the latter to preserve the country intact, its religion secure, its people in justice—and in so doing, make possible man's redemption in the afterlife. But now, the peasants felt, the state was no longer concerned with religious values and aims. It was pursuing secular power goals, and it claimed the right to prescribe the contents and forms of human existence, even to the extent of disregarding God-given injunctions (for example, that man look like Him, that is, wear a beard). Furthermore, in popular ideology, the tsar was the father of his people, he protected them, he was their high justicer—that is why he had to be accessible to all his children. After the Code of 1649, this was no longer true even legally. And since Peter the Great the situation had been aggravated by the fact that the landlord stood between tsar and people. The prohibition, repeatedly stated in decrees (most forcefully in 1767), against the peasant addressing himself directly to the tsar was clear evidence of it.

Instead of the tsar, it was the lord who held all rights over the peasant, including punishment and banishment to Siberia (only death was theoretically beyond his jurisdiction, but in practice even this was not always so). To add insult to injury, this lord intruded into the peasant's life, disregarded his traditions, imposed new dress and new ways, forced him to perform various activities which were not truly Christian or not respectable. The lord also invaded the personal life of his serfs; as their absolute master, he could cruelly beat and disfigure them, dishonor their daughters and wives, force them into marriage against their will, prevent them from performing their religious duty by working them on Sundays or Church feasts. Agents of a novel, alien, secular and rationalistic polity, the serf-owning nobility were like a new "priesthood" whose ordination was not recognized by the people. And then in 1762 the justification for the landlord's domination, that is, that he served the emperor and had to be supported by the peasantry, came to an end. If the nobleman no longer had to serve, why should the peasant remain his serf?

Peter III reinforced these feelings by his clumsy approach to the secularization of Church lands. His decree of March 21, 1762, led a credulous peasantry to believe that it was but the first step toward universal emancipation, or at least toward a general transfer of all private serfs to the state. So much more bitter was the serfs' disillusionment when Peter's decree was abrogated by Catherine II. The peasantry's restless mood was further aggravated by the increasingly frequent reimposition of corvée, which we mentioned in the section on agriculture, and by the more routine complaints about high taxes and high prices on essential commodities. Rumors were rife that a new tsar, the true Christian tsar, was coming to replace the foreign woman and to reestablish true justice (*pravda*) in the Russian land. These hopes fed on the mysterious and very sudden death of Peter III; rumor had it that he had not died, but had left the evil capital city to wander about the land, and that he was about to declare himself. Several pretenders claiming to be Peter III appeared in the late 1760s. Last, but not least, the Cossacks, as we have mentioned, particularly the Ural Host, were extremely disgruntled with their new service obligations and with the central government's interference in their traditional organization. There was also plenty of combustible material among the natives, particularly the Bashkirs, and among the factory peasants of the Urals. All these factors combined to provoke the most serious peasant uprising in imperial Russia, the Pugachev rebellion.

The revolt started on the Ural river in late summer 1773. The Don Cossack Emelian Pugachev gave himself out to be Peter III who had escaped the murderous clutches of his wife, had made a pilgrimage to the Holy Land and Constantinople, and had wandered through the Russian land for twelve years, seeing with his own eyes the plight of his people. He now revealed himself to reclaim his rightful throne and bring justice and peace to all his subjects. The Ural Cossacks, whose grievances were particularly serious and recent, joined him and constituted his staff and shock troops. Pugachev moved first against Orenburg, the capital of the Ural region, and on his way attracted a sizable number of Bashkir clans and tribes. He laid siege to the fortress of Orenburg and kept it up for several months, but was unable to take the city when rescue troops forced their way to the besieged fortress. He retreated into the Bashkir steppes and the Ural Mountains. There Pugachev spent the winter and early spring months of 1774 recruiting Ural workers and gathering an impressive artillery. In the late spring of 1774 he sallied forth from the Urals, marched to the Volga without meeting much resistance, and on the way attracted Church and factory peasants to his banner (the Bashkirs did not follow him beyond the confines of their traditional territory, although they kept up the fight against government forces). Pugachev was able to capture Kazan and several smaller towns on the middle Volga. But he could not retain control of Kazan for very long. Chased out of the city, he crossed the Volga and turned northward, apparently aiming at Nizhnii Novgorod.

At this moment the peasants rose en masse and a violent jacquerie engulfed the provinces on the western bank of the Volga. At the news of the approach of Pugachev or his lieutenants, the serfs rose against their lords, killed or chased them and their families, and burned their estates, destroying the mantelpieces and glass-paned windows of the mansions as hated symbols of an alien way of life. Armed with whatever they could lay their hands on, the serfs organized their own administration. The jacquerie spread like wildfire, and the nobles in and around Moscow panicked, started to organize their own militia, and deluged Catherine II with appeals for help. According to some memoirists, rumblings of revolt were to be heard among the peasantry around Moscow; had Nizhnii Novgorod fallen, the whole of central Russia would probably have been in the throes of the rebellion—not excluding Moscow, where the full extent of popular fear, disaffection, and primitive prejudices had been dramatically displayed during the cholera riots of 1771.

Поддинное изображение Wahre Abbildung
бунтовщика и обманщика des Rebellen und Betrügers
ЕМЕЛЬКИ ПУГАЧЕВА. IEMELKA PUGATSCEW.

The captured Pugachev

But Pugachev was apparently not interested in leading a jacquerie. Having lost the bulk of his fighting forces at Kazan, he soon abandoned the northwesterly direction he had first taken, and decided to make his way to the Don to arouse his fellow Cossacks. He descended southward on the western bank of the Volga, leaving the serfs in revolt in the central Volga provinces to their own devices and fate. Naturally, their resistance was put down without too much trouble by regular troops brought back from the Turkish war. With a handful of men, and counting on the complicity of the Cossack garrison, Pugachev tried to capture the key fortress of Tsaritsyn, but failed. At this point he was abandoned by his last followers; and his Cossack lieutenants, who had entered into negotiations with Catherine and Potemkin, turned him over to Colonel Mikhelson, commander of the pursuing forces. Pugachev was brought to Moscow in a cage, tried, and executed in January 1775. As was to be expected, the repression of his followers—Cossacks, Bashkirs, and serfs—was fierce, for the panic they had caused among the nobility and the trouble they had given Catherine's government were not easily forgiven. Thus ended the most important and last general serf uprising under the Romanovs. After 1775 all the peasant revolts, and they were still numerous in the nineteenth century up until the very eve of Emancipation, had a strictly local character. They were provoked by particular grievances and fortuitous conditions on a given estate or in a limited area. They were easily put down without spreading to a wider territory.

Let us briefly consider the main features of the Pugachev revolt and then reflect on the reasons why it was the last general serf rising, or peasant war, as the Soviets like to call it. We have pointed out that Pugachev's main fighting force were Cossacks; in a sense, except for the widespread jacquerie at the end of the revolt which Pugachev neither controlled nor commanded (he was only the pretext for its occurrence), it was more of a Cossack (and Bashkir) rising than a peasant revolt. It is nonetheless true that it was a revolt against the new, "modern" features of Russia's imperial political and social systems we have noted earlier. As Peter III, Pugachev promised the restoration of the old order that had been destroyed by St. Petersburg, especially by the evil foreigner Catherine and her henchmen. For the Cossacks, this restoration would have meant a return to their administrative autonomy and their traditional way of life; for the Bashkirs, it would have secured their right to "live [free] as animals," that is, remain nomads under their traditional customs and leaders. Pugachev also promised the restoration and free exercise of the old ritual; and most of the Cossacks, and a very high percentage of the peasants who followed him, were Old Believers. He neither gave nor promised "land and freedom"; he held to the old liturgical conception of society: every group had to serve the rightful and Christian tsar, but each did it in its own traditional way. None of the foreign, rational, bureaucratic ways of St. Petersburg were to survive if Pugachev became the ruler. That is why he passively approved, or even—in the last phase of the revolt—encouraged, the peasants to rise against the nobility, for the noble serf owners had betrayed their original purpose and raison d'être; they had ceased to be servants of the tsar. Instead, they had arrogated to themselves the right to regulate and to change the traditional ways of the peasant; they had interposed themselves between the tsar and his people; in short, they were evil and ungodly interlopers, the servants of Antichrist.

Like all primitive rebellions aiming at the restoration of the past, Pugachev's rising was bound to fail. Gradually, even the Russian peasant was losing the old ways and, however reluctantly and slowly, coming to accept the new features of national life. The old mythology lived on in folklore, but it ceased to be a dynamic force, as the Bakuninists were to find out in the second half of the nineteenth century. The Cossacks were definitively tamed after 1775; they could no longer lead a revolt, and without their military know-how and leadership, peasant revolts were bound to remain fragmented and localized. As a matter of fact, the settlement of 1775, which we mentioned in an earlier chapter, proved highly successful from the government's point of view. It secured the Cossacks against absorption by the serf peasantry and guaranteed them, especially their officers, important privileges and rewards for their military role. They became the most loyal mainstay of the imperial regime in the nineteenth century. Finally, Catherine II also drew a practical administrative lesson from the revolt. The local administration was improved effectively, and the nobility was given a larger share in it; together they saw to it that any peasant uprising would remain localized. Hence a better "*encadrement*," as the French call it, of the serf peasantry largely succeeded in neutralizing their propensity to revolt against abusive and intolerable conditions.[5]

The impact of the Pugachev revolt on Russian society and on the consciousness of its elite cannot be underestimated. It transformed the image the upper classes had of the peasantry, a subject we shall discuss at greater length in Chapter 7. The revolt forced the thoughtful members of the elite to define anew their relationship to the mass of the peasantry. In a sense, the revolt contributed to the self-definition of the Russian intelligentsia, to its sense of guilt and duty toward the people. In the average nobleman, of course, the revolt merely instilled fear; it made him more suspicious of the peasant who, he believed, had to be kept down by force. This resulted in the rank-and-file's distrust and fear of any emancipation. Yet, the problem of serfdom had been put sharply in focus by the rebellion. The government could not readily disregard it, not only in economic, but in sociopolitical terms as well. Discussions concerning the various aspects of the economy of serfdom continued after 1775, and the

[5] Although it played a very subordinate role, Catherine II and her successors tried to prevent excessive abuses by individual serf owners. In this endeavor, the rulers were given some assistance by the nobility who feared that excessive cruelty and exploitation by one of their neighbors might spark a general revolt.

Free Economic Society's concern with the peasantry did not diminish, although most of these discussions did not reach a wide public. Obviously, Catherine II was not ready to make far-reaching political changes beyond the improvement of local administration and the granting of corporate rights to the nobility.

The issue of peasant bondage did not vanish from the consciousness of the imperial government. We have mentioned that Paul I intended to circumscribe the effects of the "corvée offensive" by limiting to three a week the number of days a peasant could be forced to work his master's land. But it was Alexander I who took concrete steps with respect to serfdom. One of his early acts was to forbid publicity concerning the sale of individual serfs; he also tried to prohibit the sale of serfs separately from their family. Finally, by abrogating the nobility's monopoly over real estate ownership, he expected to spread possession of land among other classes, including freed peasants. More far-reaching in its intention was his Law on Free Agriculturists, 1803, which made it relatively easy for individual owners to take the initiative in freeing their serfs. At emancipation, the serf was to receive some land, or rights to its use, on conditions mutually agreeable to him and his lord. In fact, not many lords took advantage of the law; only 160 agreements were concluded under its provisions during the reign of Alexander I. In 1816 and 1819 the government freed the Baltic serfs, but without securing them possessions of any land. Thus the Baltic peasantry became free but landless, which resulted in its remaining economically at the mercy of the lords. The fate of the Baltic peasantry was to serve as a reminder to the Russian government, and especially to its more progressive members, that freedom without land was not very meaningful, and that henceforth any emancipation scheme had to provide for land for the freedmen. This was an additional reason for the strong resistance to general emancipation on the part of the nobility and for the long delay in carrying it out.

Serfdom continued to preoccupy Alexander I and his government even during the so-called period of reaction after 1815. Many government officials believed—and the serfs themselves wished it—that the most desirable approach was first to transfer the private serfs to the status of state peasants, while improving the administration and condition of the latter. With this notion in mind, Alexander hit upon the idea (which he had probably taken from similar institutions and projects current in the Habsburg monarchy at the end of the eighteenth century) of setting up military colonies. The plan was to work roughly as follows: peasants would be resettled in appropriate locations, given economic assistance and technical guidance from the government, and dramatically improve their material circumstances; in return, they would serve as militia in case of need. In Alexander's mind, the colonies were to be models and pioneer projects for a gradual transformation of the condition of the state peasants; eventually they would also serve to absorb the private serfs, so that one would not need to fear the political and social consequences of a general emancipation. Whatever the emperor's good intentions and the practicality of his plan, reality proved him wrong. The peasants resented the militarization of their existence. In most instances, bad execution, inefficiency, and corruption negated whatever good there may have been in the scheme. The energetic Count Arakcheev, as head of the project, earned his worst reputation by the callous ways in which he carried out his imperial master's will. Little wonder that the colonies were sorry failures, at best showpieces, whose exterior hid the misery, apathy, and helpless anger of the peasants forced into them. Far from tackling the serf problem, the colonies only aroused the indignation of progressive public opinion and provided an additional cause for the Decembrist movement.

However seriously he may have viewed the serf question, Alexander I was determined to keep its solution well within the control of the government. He did not tolerate any private initiative, especially if it was a collective one. Thus he angrily brushed aside, and threatened with his displeasure, a group of prominent noblemen who, in 1820, under the leadership of Prince Vasil'chikov, had dared to suggest a plan for a cooperative, voluntary emancipation of their serfs under the terms of the Free Agriculturists Law. The possibility of the nobility, especially its upper rungs, acting as leaders in freeing the peasantry seemed a direct threat to the Petrine tradition—to which Alexander I held firmly—that all initiative and guidance had to come from the state, more particularly from its autocratic head. This was the approach Alexander II eventually took in emancipating the serfs in 1861.

Our knowledge concerning the urban and middle classes is still too limited for us to have much to say about them. They were a small group of the population. Urban dwellers were not really a homogeneous class, since peasants, serfs who worked in towns, and nobles and officials who resided there were also included. We have seen that the municipal administration gave them little autonomy and also subjected them to a heavy burden of services and taxes. As a result, the urban community, *posadskaia obshchina*, did not develop in the course of the eighteenth century. It was very difficult, even for the more energetic, enterprising, and rich, to acquire a position of some independence and wealth. True, the farming out of the collection of taxes and of the monopoly on alcohol did result in large fortunes. But the lucky few who made the fortunes used them to secure ranks which eventually gave them titles of nobility; and they (or their children) thus joined the class of service nobility and severed all ties with the urban population. There was no bourgeoisie that could aspire to a rise in status through the professions and the *noblesse de robe*, as in France, or by acquiring land and joining the local gentry, as in England.

The Charter to the Towns of 1785 did at least create conditions of greater security for the persons and property of the wealthier merchants; it also gave them a corporate identity and some degree of autonomy. The affairs of the city were entrusted to the richer merchants, organized in three guilds, of which only the first two really counted. One joined a guild by virtue of one's declared capital; membership in the first or second guild depended on the amount so declared. As long as one owned the minimum capital required, one remained a member of the guild, enjoyed its social advantages, and participated in the municipal government. It was still a very limited participation, since ultimately the power of decision rested with the governor or other imperial officials. At any rate, many affairs that concerned the merchants' internal corporative life (for example, disputes that could be arbitrated, guardianship of orphans, supervision of bankruptcy proceedings) were now in the hands of members of the guilds. This no doubt helped to raise the image of the group in their own eyes as well as in those of the government. It also made for greater regularity of judicial and administrative procedures involving commercial, financial, and industrial assets. In short, it was a framework within which a middle class could develop. It may be added that practitioners of the free professions—unless in government service and holders of a rank—were assimilated into the top two guilds. Eventually, the special title of "named citizen" ("*imenityi grazhdanin*") was created to add some luster and status to the most successful merchants, entrepreneurs, and professionals. A start had been made, but the development did not bear fruit on a significant scale until the middle of the reign of Nicholas I.

A last group in the Russian population needs to be considered, the clery, or rather—in the Russian terminology—the spiritual (ecclesiastic) estate (*dukhovnoe soslovie*). But it is best treated in the context of Church and state relations and ecclesiastical policies in the following chapter.

6

Church and Religion

T he notion of symphony between Church and State (actually between patriarch and tsar) that had been the traditional conception in Muscovy, did, in practice, signify the predominance of the state. Only very strong personalities, under special circumstances, had secured a preponderant influence for the patriarchate. But in case of conflict, as Patriarch Nikon found out to his chagrin, the state stood the better chance of winning easily. The establishment, therefore, of the Holy Synod (1721), whatever the body's canonical status, was not so much a change in the actual relationship between Church and State as it was a revolutionary innovation in form. Thereafter, the administration of Church affairs was the responsibility of a "department" in the regular governmental structure.

Because of the preponderance that the *ober-prokurator* of the Holy Synod acquired in fact, even such strictly ecclesiastical matters as those involving the interpretation and application of canon law were not exempt from secular influence. Viewing the Church as an instrument of state power, Peter the Great went so far as to require of the priests that they report whatever they might hear in confession which might be of concern to the secular authorities. Naturally, this contributed to diminish the moral authority of the priests. On the other hand, Peter made efforts to have the clergy play a more active educational role than it had in the past: "Cipher" schools for the elementary education of all classes were to be established by the Church in all towns and larger parishes. But as the curriculum was a secular one—basically the three Rs—the clergy was neither willing nor able to assume responsibility for these institutions, and they did not strike roots in the country. A regular network of parish schools as part of the educational opportunities for the peasantry and townspeople did not develop until well into the nineteenth century. Imposing the traditional function of the Western Church as an agency of social welfare, Peter compelled monasteries to act as old age homes for invalid and retired service personnel, as orphanages, and as insane asylums. But he did not provide them with additional means for this purpose, and because there was no strong precedent for it in the practice of the Russian Church, the monasteries failed to fulfill this role satisfactorily. In fact, they tried by all means, fair or foul, to avoid this obligation.

Little wonder that the moral and social influence of the Church, as an institution, was not very great among the people. To this must be added the inadequacy of the material means available to the Church to fulfill even its limited function. Peter had established a scale of state salaries for the various church officials, but at quite a low level. It is true that these salaries were complemented by the revenue the monasteries and episcopal sees derived from their lands, but these revenues varied greatly, and some monasteries were so poor as to be unable not only to perform any social functions, but even to maintain their members decently. Corruption, ignorance, poverty, were the usual conditions encountered in monasteries as well as among the parish and diocesan clergy. The material basis of the Church was further weakened when—after several false starts—Catherine II secularized all the lands still belonging to monasteries and bishoprics. From then on, the clergy was put on a direct government salary (in addition to the meager income derived for the performance of ritual functions—for example, baptism, marriage, burial). The basic salary scale was that which Peter I had set half a century earlier, and which did not even take into account the inflationary decline in the currency. This obviously did not contribute to lifting the clergy's status in the eyes of their flocks. The parish priest depended so much on the gifts and contributions of his parishioners that at times he was little more than a beggar; in many instances, too, he turned to tilling the land himself and became practically indistinguishable from his flock. It goes without saying that under these conditions he was also ignorant, demoralized, prey to debauchery and corruption; he could not possibly be a moral guide, a teacher, a spiritual leader or comforter. He was little more than the government official who performed the Church's ritual—and even this he often did poorly and inaccurately.

The hierarchy was not in a position to remedy the situation. First of all, its ranks were filled from among the "black clergy," that is, the monks. This meant that the bishops themselves had lived and been trained in an environment isolated from both laity and parish clergy; they had no pastoral experience whatever. They made their careers on the strength of their abilities as administrators (abbots, vicars, clerks in the Holy Synod) or because of their scholarly distinction. Neither of these qualities necessarily guaranteed success when they were called upon to lead their clergy and minister to their flocks. In addition, bishops were rarely kept in one diocese for long; they were moved every few years, before they could familiarize themselves with the conditions of their diocese and become acquainted with many of their clergy (many dioceses, too, were quite extended). As their "careers" depended on the Holy Synod, they devoted their energies either to securing assignments in the synod offices or to being good at the kind of bureaucratic activities that were noticed by the synod. Of course, there were exceptions, but they were a sad minority. Most important of all, the bishops had little understanding of and concern for the plight of the parish clergy and for their pastoral shortcomings. The common people were the losers, since they received no moral or spiritual guidance. Not surprisingly, many pagan rites and superstitions, as well as errors in ritual and interpretation, survived among the populace well into the nineteenth century.

Yet in spite of its major failing in pastoral functions, the Russian Church played a not insignificant role in Russia's scholarly and cultural progress in the eighteenth and nineteenth centuries. While Peter's plan to use the Church in building a system of general and popular education failed, the ecclesiastical schools did come to make an important contribution to the Westernization of Russian culture and to the spread of learning. The basic model on which the ecclesiastical schools were built—diocesan seminaries and subsequently several ecclesiastical academies—derived from the Kievan Theological Academy of the seventeenth century. The latter, in turn, because of its exposed position in combating the proselytism of the Polish Catholic Church in the Ukraine, had adopted several features of Western Catholic learning. As a result, instruction in Russian ecclesiastical schools was given in Latin, while the languages taught besides Latin were Greek, some Hebrew, and Church Slavonic. The emphasis was on scholastic philosophy, logic, and dogmatic theology. The methods of teaching were "scholastic" in the pejorative sense, that is, syllogistic analysis, summary and restatements of arguments and conclusions. Later in the eighteenth century more modern subjects were added, namely, a smattering of German and French, some natural science, and more ecclesiastical history. The philosophy curriculum was also modernized with the introduction of contemporary German philosophy, especially that of Christian Wolff. All this did not prepare the seminarian for the pastorate; the practice sermons and speeches were given in Latin, so that a bishop later recalled that he did not know how to preach in Russian and had to write his sermon first in Latin and then translate it. The seminary training did, however, provide the graduates with intellectual tools that were of great use in administration, since they learned how to handle documents, analyze and excerpt them, and how to write summaries and draft arguments. To the talented and ambitious seminarians, there were two careers open: taking Holy Orders, they could rise in the hierarchy (by way of scholarship or administration, or both); but this did not appeal to everyone. The other career was service in the state administration, although it was not always easy, for example, under Elizabeth and Paul, to obtain the required release from the ecclesiastic estate. Many followed this path, and some rose quite high and even attained nobility.

The state allotted a ridiculously small budget for the upkeep of the ecclesiastical schools. Appalling conditions prevailed in the schools as a result of the government's niggardliness: The students were forced to beg for their upkeep; they fell victim to disease and malnutrition; they were demoralized and debauched. Only the hardiest, luckiest, and ablest could survive and profit from such a regimen. Another serious defect was that their curriculums had not kept pace with intellectual developments since the seventeenth century. The major reforms introduced in 1808 under the energetic leadership of Speransky, himself a seminary and academy graduate, for the first time provided the schools with a solid, although by no means lavish, material foundation: The revenue from the sale of the wax candles placed before the icons in the churches went for the upkeep of the ecclesiastical schools. The curriculum was modernized and improved: Russian became the normal language of instruction, modern languages (mainly French) were to be taught, greater attention was to be given to natural sciences (physics, chemistry, biology) and mathematics. Finally, the ecclesiastical subjects were made more relevant for a future clergyman's duties, more emphasis being put on practice preaching, homiletics, the history of the Church. The philosophical orientation, too, was modernized; not only Wolff, but also Locke and Kant were to be studied.

Although the fruits of this reform were not evident until the second quarter of the nineteenth century, the ecclesiastical schools did become solid educational institutions. And because the student body was drawn from the impoverished and ambitious children of the clergy (with a sprinkling of merchants or townspeople), it is not surprising that the schools were the seedbed for professionals and academics. Indeed, as a glance at the list of university professors and at the rolls of Russian science, technology, and medicine will show, the overwhelming majority of those active in these fields around the middle of the nineteenth century were graduates of the ecclesiastical seminaries and academies. In this indirect and some-what paradoxical way, the Church contributed to the Europeanization of Russia culture, as well as to the spread of Western intellectual influences, including philosophical materialism. It had renewed for nineteenth-century Russia the function of the medieval Western church as one of the founts of scholarship and science. This ac-complishment, however, did not contribute to its effectiveness as the spiritual and moral guide of the common people.

In view of these circumstances, the active religious life of both the common people and educated classes took place, in the main, out-side the institutional framework of the official Church. Attendance at services, yearly communion, and the like were formalities per-formed because they were required by custom and by the govern-ment; but they did not involve the soul; they did not satisfy the spiritual needs of those who yearned for a meaningful religious life. The yearning for greater spiritual and religious significance was very strong among the people and the elite, probably because of the questioning and conflict that had become manifest as a result of Russia's rapid transformation and Europeanization in the eighteenth century. At the end of the century, and continuing into the first quarter of the nineteenth, there was an intense and profound religious revival.

The revival took place in the context of individual experience and under the influence of teachings from the West, particularly German Pietism. Its aim was to heighten the intensity and meaning of per-sonal religious experience, and to help others to attain it. This obviously was coming close to mysticism, so that we often find this revival taking the form traditional in the Eastern Church of a per-sonal and socially directed mysticism (Hesychasm and kenosis). Frequently this occurred in response to the example set by some influential *starets* (holy man); such was the role played by St. Tik-hon Zadonsky. Another example was G. Skovoroda who, in a more secular and eclectic vein, drew his inspiration from Plato as much as from the mystical tradition of the Russian Church and the Pietist teachings. Known as the Ukrainian Socrates, Skovoroda taught more by his own example and his ascetic, wandering life than by his writ-ings, which did not become well known until much later in the nine-teenth century. Freemasonry, too—especially in its mystical and philanthropic orientations—was close to this revival. Its leaders, J. G. Schwarz and especially N. I. Novikov and A. Labzin, were deeply religious men for whom membership in the lodge and activity on behalf of their fellow-men were only the visible expressions of genuine piety and an individual religious search.

The political events of the late eighteenth and early nineteenth centuries, in Russia as well as in Europe, obviously heightened the need many felt for religious answers to personal and national problems. Under the impact of the catastrophic invasion of Napoleon, and partaking of the general spiritual revival of the period, members of the Russian upper class experienced a wave of mysticism often touched with spiritualism (for instance, in the circle of Princess Tatarinova). Alexander I himself set an example by his closeness to the exalted Christianity of Mme de Krüdener, his sponsorship of the Holy Alliance, and the obscurantist-mystical orientation he gave to cultural policies after 1815. Even the rationalistically inclined generation of the Decembrists manifested serious and strong religious concerns, though they did not take mystical or pietistic form. The Masonic lodges that were revived or founded after 1815 had a stronger mystical element than did the lodges of Catherine's time. Related to the progressive elite's interest in religion, and quite distinct from the spiritualism and conservative mysticism (of Arkhimandrit Fotii's stripe), was the popularity and official sponsorship of the Bible Society. Quite clearly, in view of the official Church's failure to provide meaningful religious guidance, it was necessary to go back to the very source of Christianity, the Scriptures. The English Bible Society, under the patronage of Alexander I, did much to popularize the reading of the Scriptures among the educated classes, even if it was not altogether successful in spreading the Book among the illiterate peasantry; it was instrumental in bringing about the completion and publication of a translation of the New Testament into the Russian vernacular. Finally, in some circles of the upper nobility in close contact with French emigrés, a series of conversions to Catholicism occurred. The conversions took place in a Pietistic mood, largely under the influence of the Jesuits whom Catherine II had admitted to Russia after the dissolution of their order, and under the intellectual guidance of J. de Maistre. The number of conversions to Roman Catholicism was small, but it affected distinguished and influential families, and it further demonstrated the almost universal need for a more meaningful religious experience, an experience the Russian Church was incapable of providing.

As far as the common people were concerned, personally meaningful religious life was most frequently to be found in the Old Belief and its various offshoots. In spite of the persecutions to which they were subjected, the number of Old Believers did not diminish. They had been brutally repressed by Peter the Great, in whom they saw the Antichrist and to whom they refused obedience; they escaped into the forests or immolated themselves rather than shave their beards and accept conscription or pay taxes. Many fled across the border to Poland and the lower Danube. The repression was not relaxed after Peter; it was Catherine II who finally acquiesced to a *modus vivendi* under which the Old Believers, although discriminated against by law, were in fact left alone. Under Elizabeth, too, some attempts were made to bring the Old Believers back into the fold, but with very limited success. In the latter part of the eighteenth century various sects, mostly of a fundamentalist and mystical orientation, spread among the common people. Many were offshoots of Old Believer communities, especially from those that had remained priestless, since they did not recognize ordinations by regular Orthodox bishops. Some other sects seem to have arisen under the influence of contacts with Protestantism, especially Pietism (*shtundists, molokane*). In brief, the religious ferment was as great among the peasantry, the common people, as among the educated, although with the former it was more revivalist and quite confused with respect to creed and dogma. Catherine II took a relatively tolerant attitude; while her government did what it could to check the spread of these sects, it did not actively persecute them. The policy of tolerance was continued by Alexander I, who was more concerned about the upper classes than he was about the religious seekings of the common people.

In conclusion, a few words are in order concerning Church policy with respect to the non-Christian subjects of the empire. Peter the Great did not encourage missionary activity on the part of the Church; Empresses Anna and Elizabeth, however, did. They supported the aggressive efforts of the archbishops of Kazan to convert the various Finnish tribes on the Volga (Cheremiss, Mordva, Chuvash). Aided by local officials, their efforts resulted in most of these primitive tribes accepting Christianity for fear of reprisals, but without fully understanding the tenets of their new religion. As a matter of fact, the drive for conversion was far from being disinterested, for after baptism the natives were subject to the capitation and could be enserfed more easily. The new converts became the object of shameless and brutal exploitation: Since they did not know or understand their new religion, they frequently violated its practices (or could easily be misled into doing so). This brought upon them the wrath of the clergy, and they then had to buy themselves free from severe punishment. Conversion thus became a source of exploitation and corruption by local clerical and secular authorities. The central government was either ignorant or unwilling to intervene. Little wonder that these natives followed Pugachev into rebellion and that their conversion remained formal and superficial.

Similar efforts directed at the Muslims, especially the Tartars of the Volga, were less successful. Few actually converted, but in the process many mosques and schools were destroyed, the feelings of the Tartars badly hurt, and their loyalty strained to the breaking point. Catherine II ordered a lessening of the conversion drive and followed a more tolerant religious policy, even though she still hoped to bring about the cultural russification of the Muslim Tartars. In short, while not very successful in terms of the number of actual conversions, the policy of the Church did arouse much discontent and contributed to the emergence of the nationality question later in the nineteenth century. It is significant to note, however, that the Church could pursue its missionary activities only as long as they were also supported by the state. If the government or the monarch were neutral or uninterested, the Church had little authority and few means to do the job on its own. Here, too, its subordination to state interests and policies was quite obvious.

Protestants enjoyed full freedom to have their churches and to practice their ritual. Lutheranism remained the official recognized church of the Baltic provinces and in Finland. The situation of Roman Catholicism was a little more complicated. Foreign Catholics were tolerated and had their churches in the capitals, but the government was careful not to allow the Catholic Church to proselytize in the Ukraine and the Western provinces (after their annexation). Although Catherine II set up the archbishopric of Mohilev for the Catholics (St. Siestrzencewicz-Bohusz held this post throughout our period), she kept its activities and clergy under strict control. In this period, too, the Catholic Church was little interfered with in occupied Poland. The Russian government was always careful not to permit conversions to Catholicism and, before the partitions, strongly discouraged the sending of children of West Russian nobles to Catholic schools. All in all, official attitudes to Catholicism were strictly a matter of international politics, since the Catholic Church was closely connected with Rome and other Catholic powers. Unquestionably, Catholicism was discriminated against, since the state feared the political implications of Catholic inroads in the Western provinces and in the Ukraine. Paul I, after he became Grand Master of the Order of St. John of Jerusalem, and Alexander I were more tolerant of the Catholic religion, but they prohibited as strictly as their predecessors any proselytizing activities and conversions. The few conversions among the upper nobility we have mentioned earlier were sources of great scandal and often resulted in the convert's having to leave the capital.

Education and Intellectual Life

Rᵤₛₛᵢₐₙ*intellectual life was so intimately linked to the political, social, and economic evolution of the country that it can hardly be treated separately. The main reason for this was that the educated elite belonged to the Establishment, in contrast to the situation that was to prevail from the reign of Nicholas I on. In the eighteenth century the elite actively helped the government in introducing and applying to Russian life Western culture and values.

In the realm of intellectual life, Peter's injunction may be summarized in the following terms: Russia's Westernization is the goal; the spread of technology, knowledge, and education are the means; the benefit that the former will yield to the state and to society is the purpose. These were also the ideas disseminated and developed by the principal "intellectuals," the first emperor's contemporaries and associates. The term "Westernization" carried only a limited set of implications for Peter and his collaborators, since they did not conceive it to mean the destruction of the Russian character of the country. It merely meant a higher level of economic life, greater power for the state, social and cultural independence for the individual, and the participation of Russia in the political life of the West. The proportion between "foreign" and "native" elements in this mixture was hard to determine, which is why the question of Westernization eventually became a matter of such lively and fertile debate. It was also the reason why the Russians could view objectively much of what was happening in the contemporary West.

*Passages within asterisks in this chapter will appear in the forthcoming *Cambridge Guide to Russian Studies*, to be published by the Cambridge University Press, and are reproduced here with the permission of the Syndics of the Cambridge University Press.

The personalities of Ivan Pososhkov (1652–1726) and Feofan Prokopovich (1681–1736) are characteristic of the generation of transition, that is, of those who had made theirs the direction shown by Peter, but whose conceptual framework and tools of expression still belonged to the previous age. Himself a merchant and entrepreneur, Pososhkov was primarily concerned with the economic development of the country. Economic progress involved the modernization of its social organization and administration. In a way, Pososhkov went even further than Peter, for he realized clearly that these advances would be best accomplished by the merchant class and would be largely built on the prosperity of the entire population, and of the peasants in particular. It would require a government whose primary concern was the maintenance of justice and order to protect the property and security of those actively engaged in economic enterprise, the creators of goods. The passive notion of government, the primacy of justice (as well as the religious terms in which he wrote) mark Pososhkov as belonging in some respects to an earlier, medieval, framework of political and social thought. His purpose, however, was the achievement of a high level of material welfare for all, and in this regard he was the harbinger of a new orientation in Russia's social development.

The role which Pososhkov played in the domain of economic thought and material progress Feofan Prokopovich played in the realm of political theory and religious affairs. He was the main architect of the new Church settlement predicated on the priority of the secular aims of the state and on the subordination of the Church to the role of the state's handmaid. In his political theory, Prokopovich was the principal exponent and best advocate of unlimited royal power that would enable the monarch to perform his political tasks and fulfill his obligations to the nation. In his famous treatise, *Pravda voli monarshei* (*The Justice of the Monarch's Will*, 1722), he defended the notion that the ruler was God on earth, that he had to be obeyed under all circumstances. The interesting implication was that this submission was necessary to promote the material welfare of the people and to foster their secular happiness. He used with great effectiveness Hobbes' argument that the social contract necessarily required that the ruler have absolute power, for the sake of preserving the life of the individual and of society.

In making the Church an instrument of the state, especially with respect to its educational function, Prokopovich followed in the footsteps of the German Protestant state churches and found support in references to natural law doctrine. Like Pososhkov, however, he could not shed his earlier theological training and manner of exposition. His writings are replete with scholastic rhetoric and a reliance on exegesis and illustration from the Scriptures. Conscious of the vital role education had to play in promoting rational attitudes which in turn would benefit both the state and society, this unusual prelate became a great propagandist of secular education, learning, and literature. In Novgorod, where he was archbishop, he established a model school with an essentially secular curriculum. He was the animator of an informal group of "intellectuals," the "learned host" ("*uchenaia druzhina*"), which played a seminal role in the propagation of the new outlook to which Peter's reforms had given initial impulse. Besides Prokopovich, the main figures of this learned host were Antiokh Kantemir (1708–1744) and V. N. Tatishchev (1686–1750).

As their first task, the learned host set themselves to propagandize the value of secular learning and modern Western rationalism. Of course, this meant popularizing the most recent scientific theories concerning the cosmos and the moral universe. This was the essential contribution of Kantemir's poetic work and of his translations. As well as aiming at shaping the Russian language into a new poetic vehicle, Kantemir's poetry had the didactic purpose of defending learning and secular knowledge, and of satirizing the social and moral shortcomings of his uncouth contemporaries. Kantemir, like the early Renaissance writers in Germany and France, thus began the Russian tradition of the social role of literature and the didactic function of criticism and poetry. In his most important work of translation, Fontenelle's *Discours sur la pluralité des mondes*, he endeavored to acquaint the Russian public with contemporary Western cosmological notions and to destroy the still-prevailing traditional medieval beliefs. He also defended a mild metaphysical materialism and was probably the first (and for a long time the only and almost unknown) Russian follower of Newton and Locke. All this made him a figure of the Enlightenment, in the Western European eighteenth-century meaning of the term.

His friend and contemporary Tatishchev pursued similar goals, but mainly in the realm of mundane affairs and in scholarship. He was first a scientist and technician, and then became a prominent administrator, particularly active in developing mining in the Urals. These activities led him to become one of the first scientific geographers and geologists in Russia; in this field, M. V. Lomonosov was to be his worthy successor. This work in turn led him to history, where he pioneered in collecting, digesting, and presenting the evidence of chronicles, and wrote what was the first modern scholarly history of Russia. Not surprisingly, like his imperial master, he was a tireless propagandist of education and secular learning. He based his philosophy and cosmology on arguments derived from natural law and subjected to rational criticism religious beliefs, superstitions, and traditions. The most comprehensive statement of his purpose and philosophy is to be found in the *Dialogue of Two Friends on the Value of Learning.* The *Dialogue* helped to give wide circulation in Russia to the corpus of Western classical and modern philosophy, especially the work of contemporary German academic philosophers who derived from Leibniz. In 1730 he defended the anti-oligarchic position of the rank-and-file nobility with arguments drawn from natural law social contract doctrines, along the lines suggested earlier by his friend Prokopovich. These three "fledglings of Peter's nest" were convinced that the educated elite's only duty was state service, for the Petrine state was the leader and guide in modernizing and developing their country and nation.

As had been true of Northwestern Europe in early Renaissance times, the generation of slavish imitators of foreign models was followed by men who endeavored to give the new acquisitions a national form, as well as to place them within the nation's traditions. Their efforts brought about the discovery of the historical, social, and economic reality of Russia. It may be said of Russia, as of Germany for example, that the rediscovery of the homeland was but a sign of the complete assimilation of foreign influences. Quite naturally, the process first helped fashion a new means of literary expression, a flexible language capable of conveying the new ideas and of describing new things and feelings. In Russia this was largely the work of M. V. Lomonosov (1711–1765), V. K. Tred'iakovsky (1703–1769), and a generation later of A. P. Sumarokov (1718–1777), G. R. Derzhavin (1743–1816), and D. I. Fonvizin (1745–1792). A by-product was the rediscovery of the old classics of the Russian language and literature, and through them the rediscovery of the country's history and of the people's particular characteristics. It brought forth a naïve and arrogant nationalism. In the realm of language and literature, this nationalism is illustrated by Lomonosov's praise of the Russian language so reminiscent of Du Bellay's *Défense et illustration.* In the domain of history, we find this desire to enhance the national glories and virtues in the works of M. M. Shcherbatov (1733–1790) and I. N. Boltin (1735–1792).

As a historian, Shcherbatov was primarily patriotic and nationalistic. But he was also a prominent publicist and political writer. The burden of his message was that the nobility was the most glorious and important class of the realm, that it should be given a position of privilege and authority commensurate with this status, a status earned by long and faithful service to the state. But the purpose of the nobility's privileged status was to encourage it to continue to play a leadership role in economic and cultural life, as well as in administrative and military affairs. Shcherbatov's traditionalism was actually directed toward a modern goal: the cultural and economic progress of Russia along the lines of individual enterprise and competitive activity. He thus made Peter's goals his own, although he believed they would work for the benefit of his class primarily. A similar ambivalence is reflected in his estimate of the pre-Petrine past. He exalted seventeenth-century Russian society for its moral virtues, but he violently denounced its ignorance and passivity. He bemoaned the decline of public morals (especially at court) since Peter, yet he refused to sacrifice the benefits of modernization. He acknowledged that on its own, without the impetus of Peter, seventeenth-century Russian society would not have reached the high level of culture, enlightenment, and power it enjoyed under Catherine II. The entire conflict of the Russian elite was expressed in this ambivalent reaction to Peter: he had broken with the past too sharply, and in so doing thrown out much that was good; yet, without him, there might not have been the progress and rapprochement with Western Europe that had been so beneficial for Russia.*

So far we have considered writers and ideas that were focused on the new state, its role and nature, and that concerned themselves only incidentally with either the individual or the people as the passive objects of the state's actions. The writings of the men we have considered, however, would not have had any impact if there had not been a parallel emergence of an educated elite in Russian society, a development that was due to the spread of education and to the content of the educational experience.

Education and even learning had existed in Muscovy, but they had been focused on religious concerns and were disseminated on an individual basis by clerks or church readers. There was no educational system in any meaningful sense of the word. It was Peter the Great who introduced secular schooling of the European type. He did it primarily in order to meet his own needs for technically trained personnel to operate the ships and maneuver the army he had created, but he saw beyond these immediate needs and was well aware that the new state would require a permanent plentiful pool of educated men to continue the work of modernization he had begun. He was equally conscious of the fact that Russia would need an educated national elite if the empire was to be as powerful and as flourishing a center of culture and military arts as he hoped. The first school he created was the Academy of Mathematics in Moscow, later transferred to St. Petersburg and renamed the Academy of Navigation; its name clearly reflected the practical purpose for which it had been founded. As we have seen, Peter also wanted to establish a network of primary schools to be administered by the Church. We know that the experiment did not succeed because the clergy was unwilling to teach secular subjects; but it also failed because the average nobleman was not yet convinced of the necessity of education.

Peter I tied the obligation to serve to that of obtaining an education, for obviously officers and administrators had to have a minimum of secular education. Because of this connection, and its compulsory nature, the idea of education was quite unwelcome to a service nobility that had no tradition of valuing learning. There was a great deal of resistance and avoidance of what appeared the most burdensome duty of all, schooling. Anecdotal history has fastened on the many comical and pathetic examples of school avoidance on the part of children of the service nobility, and on Peter's harsh measures to force compliance—retrieving runaways and truants with the help of soldiers, fining parents who abetted truancy, prohibiting marriage before completion of school. No doubt, these situations did occur, but it has often been forgotten that within one generation, the educational requirement was taken for granted by the nobility and its avoidance became a rare exception. Within less than two generations, as we have seen, the nobility even demanded that the state provide more opportunities for easy access to education. The main reason for this rapid change in attitude was the fact that service remained compulsory and the nobles' principal occupation, and that for a successful career, education was the most desirable prerequisite. Furthermore, as the demands of 1730 indicated, the nobles had realized that exemptions could be claimed from the unpleasant first stage of service as simple private or sailor on the basis of one's educational level. So education became the hallmark of the nobleman, as well as the guarantee of his privileged position in service.

Inasmuch as the legal notion of nobility, connected with the Table of Ranks, remained rather indeterminate, and the class open to access by outsiders, education was, by the middle of the eighteenth century, one of the chief criteria for belonging to the elite. As a consequence, however, the nature of education and of its aim underwent a great shift. Peter's educational orientation had been technological and utilitarian (the social graces, too, were taught for utilitarian purposes); even the Academy of Sciences (founded in 1725) had originally received this pragmatic bent. The founding of the Corps of Cadets (1731) marked a departure from this strictly utilitarian orientation not so much by its curriculum (modeled on that of German *Ritterakademien*, it emphasized preparation for a military career), as by the new atmosphere that prevailed in it. A privileged school for the select nobility, located in the capital, its students were eagerly received in good society and at court. The cadets developed new cultural aspirations—to be leaders of an elegant and stimulating social and intellectual life. They acquired a keen interest in things of the mind of Western origin, especially the more graceful and beautiful ones, such as literature, drama, music. The Corps of Cadets thus served as an early center for the translation of Western literature; its students put on the first secular dramas for St. Petersburg society; it was the locale of the first literary circles. More and more, the development of the individual's spirit and the opening up of his intellectual potential became the goal of education. Not only was schooling to prepare the young nobleman for an active life in the service of the state, but it was also to develop him into a more valuable individual, intellectually active and spiritually alive. The pattern set by the Corps of Cadets was followed by other state institutions as well as by private boarding schools and, to the extent that it was feasible, by private tutors.

By the middle of the century, education for education's sake, for the sake of general intellectual development, had been fully accepted and was taken for granted. The foundation of the University of Moscow (1755) was an illustration of the new trend.[1] Not that the university proved an immediate success as an institution of higher learning and a center for preparation for a life of the mind, of scholarship, or of science. The beginnings were difficult and slow, and the fact that attendance and graduation had only indirect bearing on promotion in the Table of Ranks or in furthering one's service career precluded the university from enjoying the popularity it was to acquire later. In spite of these limitations and of the difficulty in recruiting a good student body (as well as keeping a good faculty), the university gradually implanted in Russian society the notion of the value of intellectual training and scholarship for their own sake. It also served as a major vehicle for the transmission of new ideas in the realm of law and philosophy to a growing circle of Russians, especially after boarding schools for nobles and commoners were attached to the university. Eventually, provision was also made that a course of study at the university, and particularly graduation, would secure a higher starting rank in government service. By the early 1800s, young nobles from the provinces or from Moscow attended the university as a matter of course, unless they were admitted to the Corps of Cadets.

[1] M. V. Lomonosov was the *spiritus rector* of the enterprise, while Ivan Shuvalov was the official sponsor and first curator of the university.

I. I. Betskoy

From the technical and professional training of the military officer, the focus of education shifted to the formation of an educated, intelligent member of society, a cultural leader of his nation. Naturally, this could not be accomplished by imparting only factual information or by developing the mind alone. The whole man had to be molded and directed in his development—the life of the heart and the moral sense, as well as the intellect, had to be involved. This was the new pedagogical orientation offered in the reign of Catherine II by the state boarding schools, such as the Corps of Cadets, which was reformed along these lines, and the school for noble girls, the Smol'nyi Institute, as well as by a host of private boarding and day schools. The new pedagogical trend was promoted and executed by I. I. Betskoy, Catherine's major advisor on matters of education. Following Locke's ideas on education, and more significantly those popularized by Rousseau, Betskoy conceived the school as the place where a new man would be created, a man whose moral qualities would equal his mental equipment. Aware of the baneful influence of a family environment in which the parents were uneducated and the children left to the supervision of ignorant, superstitious, demoralized serf *nianias* and *diad'kas*, such as was common in the provinces, Betskoy believed that the only way to form a new man was by withdrawing the child from this environment altogether. He therefore advocated taking the child at a very early age (not later than six) and putting him in a boarding school, where he would remain for ten years of schooling without returning to his family even for summer vacations. In the school, under the guidance and supervision of a staff chosen as much for their moral qualities as for their knowledge, the child would develop the qualities of mind and heart that would turn him into a dedicated, responsible citizen, a true son of the fatherland, devoting his life and energies to the service of sovereign, country, and fellow-man. This program was infused with a strong Christian, Pietistic spirit that emphasized the duty of work and concern for the welfare of the community rather than the satisfaction of selfish interests.

Naturally, the reality of the educational system reformed by Betskoy fell short of this ideal. But the high goal remained, and in many cases brought beneficial results along the lines he envisioned. The new pedagogical pattern served to familiarize the Russian elite with high moral goals and spiritual aspirations, so that many a private school or tutor endeavored to follow the same precepts with respect to his charges. The Betskoy program paralleled the new intellectual orientation of the educated nobility, as well as the moral and religious bent of the Masons. Together they contributed to the successful creation of such early nineteenth-century seedbeds of the intellectual elite as the Boarding School for Nobles at the University of Moscow or the boarding schools attached to gymnasiums in the provinces (for example, in Kazan). Finally, Catherine II tried to extend these basic principles of pedagogy to the education of serfs, especially those who were destined by their masters to become tutors and caretakers of children of the nobility. The results in this case, however, were quite meager, and Catherine failed to bring into being a system of primary schools for the whole empire. In any event, the notion that the function of education was the creation of a new kind of man and the development of his moral potential took firm hold among the Russian elite. It continued to shape the basic attitudes and the concrete goals of the Russian educational system throughout the nineteenth century.

It is time to turn to the ideas and attitudes that permeated the educated elite as a result of schooling and the spread of education.

The dissemination of this new knowledge was accomplished not only by the few schools we have mentioned and through the efforts of tutors and private schools; it was also the result of translation programs, journalism, and study trips to Western universities (primarily German) undertaken by an increasingly larger number of young Russians, sent either by the government or by their parents to complete their education. Contrary to what is frequently believed, the major intellectual influence on Russia in the eighteenth century was not that of France and the French Enlightenment. This is not to deny this influence altogether (we shall return to it below); but it is essential to remember that throughout most of this century, and for most of the service nobility, German was the major foreign language. French penetrated only in the last third of the century, and even then it was mainly the preserve of the court nobility, of high society in the capital; it became the primary foreign language for the average nobleman only in the nineteenth century. For the small class of professionals and academics, German remained the primary language of communication with the outside world even in the middle of the nineteenth century. The first influence—in terms of both time and importance—was that of German thought, scholarship, and even literature. We must therefore first deal with the impact of the German *Aufklärung*, its character and its role.

Without going into the differences and peculiar characteristics of the *Aufklärung* as compared to the French Enlightenment, let us merely list the major elements of this body of ideas that proved particularly attractive to the Russians and the reasons for this attraction. The first element to be absorbed was the doctrine of natural law as it was expounded by German academic philosophers and jurists, especially those of the school of Wolff and Baumeister. The most popular Russian textbook adaptation of these notions was that of F. H. Strube de Pyrmont. Natural law doctrine appealed to the Russians because of its implicit belief in the uniformity of all men and of the fundamental principles of their conduct, so that the Russians, too, although they were not yet fully westernized, were regulated by them. Russia, it was felt, was thereby automatically put on a level of equality with the more advanced Western civilizations and peoples. But the important thing to note is that the German interpretation of natural law—besides giving a larger role to Christianity—differed from the Anglo-French version in another major aspect: It stressed not so much man's rights, as his duties and obligations to society. The individual was never seen in isolation and independently from the group; he was not endowed with absolute and equal rights. The German philosophers and jurists of the *Aufklärung* always conceived of the individual within the context of a community, with rights being conferred on him only in return for the fulfillment of his obligations to his fellow-men and to the group. Such a doctrine was not only quite acceptable to the autocratic state of Peter's creation, but also corresponded to the service orientation of the Russian nobility, to their ideal of dedication and obligation to the community and the state. It also touched a responsive chord in men raised in the tradition of Russian Orthodoxy, itself more community-centered than Roman Catholicism. This German tradition of natural law, as it was derived from Pufendorff and Leibniz, was particularly well suited to the development of notions of social responsibility that were to find their fullest expression in the doctrines of social rights. At first reinforcing the ethos of state service, the German version of natural law principles was to serve, as we shall see, to direct the attention of educated Russians to their obligations toward the people and to develop their social consciousness.

Closely related to this natural law tradition was the influence of Neostoicism which had found its institutional application in the armies shaped by the military revolution of the seventeenth century. Neostoicism too assumed the basic uniformity of all men and therefore the possibility for all cultures and nations to participate in one truly universal civilization based on natural law. In addition, it also stressed man's duty—whatever the difficulties—to live up to his obligations as a human being in society. Little wonder that it was the ethical basis of the modern army, for it also implied an acceptance of one's fate, of one's obligation to perform in the best manner possible the duty dictated by one's condition and station in life. This philosophy naturally served to reinforce the notions of duty and obedience to the state, the bearer and expression of the universal law; it also stressed the individual's obligation to participate actively in the common task of culture and civilization. The universality of ethical principles and of the notion of culture appealed— as it had to the barbarians in the Late Roman Empire—to a nation that was attempting to join the ranks of "universal civilization." At the same time, the Neostoic emphasis on the will, its voluntaristic bent, was particularly attractive to members of a service group who felt they were in the process of creating a modern state and society.

This voluntaristic component also reinforced the belief held by the Russian elite that man was capable, by dint of his own effort, not only of creating himself spiritually, but also of creating the kind of society he aspired to. Membership in the service class, in the educated elite, therefore required not merely obedience to the moral authority of the state and acknowledgment of its great power; it also demanded active, conscious, and willful participation in the creative process of shaping the new man and the best social framework for him. Hence the Russian elite's belief in the creative role of law—for example, S. Desnitsky and Ia. Kozel'sky—which also took the form of a belief in legislation and codification as the vehicles for the transformation of society and culture, for the creation of a new human and spiritual order. The voluntaristic element naturally appealed to an elite that had developed a strong social consciousness and that was anxious to act on its new insight to transform Russian reality. Little wonder that in the late eighteenth and early nineteenth centuries, civic-minded poets—Pnin and Radishchev, for instance—so frequently stressed man's almost infinite ability to forge himself and his environment.

Another important aspect of German *Aufklärung* thought that had a profound impact on Russia in the eighteenth century was Pietism, as it was propagated by merchants, doctors, and teachers trained in H. Francke's institutions at Halle. Incidentally, it was also to Halle that a number of Russian students were sent in the course of the century, especially in the early years. Although the missionary zeal of Pietist men of letters, scholars, merchants, and professionals did not lead to conversions, it instilled into the life and thought of the Russian educated class a strong religious component. Pietism helped to bring about the change in religious attitudes described in the previous chapter. Dissatisfied with the inadequacies of institutionalized religion in Russia, the more sophisticated and searching souls found in the Pietist stress on the personal moral and spiritual aspects of religion an answer that filled their need without forcing them to give up their formal membership in the official Church. Pietism emphasized action and a stoic stance with respect to external circumstances; consequently, it gave a high value to social responsibility and involvement. Not surprisingly, many a Russian who had sought a personal and meaningful religious experience and had been impressed by the Pietist approach discovered the full implications of his obligations and duty to his fellow-men. He followed up this realization with a genuine commitment to social action and philanthropy.

The religious search and the discovery of one's obligation to one's fellow-men naturally led to spiritualistic and philanthropic freemasonry. Its popularity in Russia can be easily explained by the fact that it served the spiritual needs of a class that had been raised in the tradition of service. Within the framework of freemasonry, the educated nobleman found it possible to combine his religious quest with his urge to act and serve his fellow-men. Under the leadership and inspiration of I. Schwarz and Novikov, the Freemasons undertook a number of voluntary and independent campaigns to help the sick and the starving during famine, to educate the poor, to spread good literature by setting up lending libraries, publishing houses, and translation circles, both in Moscow and in the provinces. The Masons ran afoul of Catherine II because she was suspicious of activities involving social reform that were carried out without state supervision and guidance. As important as this general consideration may have been, however, her general distrust of the secrecy and ritual of the Masons, and their personal connection with the heir, Grand Duke Paul, led her to dissolve the lodges and arrest, investigate, and exile the leaders of the Moscow Masonic circles, Novikov, Ivan Turgenev, and Labzin (Schwarz had died previously).

Another equally important contribution of Pietism was to pave the way for sentimentalism. As an attitude, sentimentalism emphasized the importance of the heart, of emotion, and proclaimed that every human being, however low his station in life, even a serf, had emotions and a life of the heart as valuable and as valid as that of the highest-born nobleman. As far as Russia was concerned, Pietism much more than Rousseau stimulated a new view of emotion; namely, the view that no human activity was truly of value unless it came as the result of a passionate involvement, a profound emotional and spiritual commitment. Moreover, emotions and passions of this kind are common to all men. It may be interesting to note in passing that Russian sentimentalism owes as much, if not more, to translations and popularizations of second-rate German sentimental literature as to the great English sentimental writers Sterne and Gray, who were usually known to Russians through German translations. Sentimentalism helped to prepare the ground for a new image of the peasant and a concern for his fate; at the same time, it endowed other intellectual influences from the West with an emotional cast, a dynamic quality of moral passion and commitment that turned them into guides and instruments of action rather than of analysis and understanding. This is the reason why it was important that the ideas of the French Enlightenment came to Russia at the same time as, or immediately after, the impact of the *Aufklärung* had been fully absorbed. This circumstance gave the ideas of the Enlightenment a different dynamic tone than they had originally had in the West.

The French influence was primarily a literary one. French literature was translated and read, particularly in the capital and in court circles, but it was mainly a source of entertainment (which did not exclude a broadening of the mental and cultural horizon of the readers). Through this literature, information on the life of European high society penetrated into Russia and generated a desire to emulate its elegance, amusements, and leisure. It was also their success as entertainment that accounts for the popularity of Voltaire's novels and tales. True, they did stimulate skepticism and some anti-ecclesiastical feeling, but the latter was never an important element in Russian life and thought, since the Church itself was such a weak institution. The Russians did not share the epistemological interests of the *philosophes*; Kantemir was the only important writer who had been interested in epistemology, but in this respect he had no followers for almost a century. Neither was the *philosophes'* critique of Western conditions relevant to Russia. As for the notions of individualism and natural rights, they could neither be easily adapted to Russian reality, nor displace the rival claims of the German *Aufklärung*—more conservative, but more relevant to Russian circumstances.[2]

Of course, the ideas of the *philosophes* were bound to make an impact, eventually. But the full impact came late in the century and with Rousseau leading the way, for Rousseau had strong affinities with the *Aufklärung* tradition we have discussed. He found the ground prepared for his ideas, since he too stressed the importance of shaping a new man possessing the right feelings and moral passion, a socially conscious and actively committed member of society. Along with Rousseau came the influence of the more radical later generation of *philosophes*—Holbach, Helvetius, and especially Raynal—with whom Russians had become acquainted abroad. Their impact was strong, since they stressed the need for action and the notions of social rights and responsibilities, while Raynal played heavily on the emotions in his plea against slavery and the evils of exploitation. The sentimental bourgeois moralism and radicalism of the late Enlightenment converged with the philosophical and religious impact of the *Aufklärung*. Thus, from the very start, the role of the French Enlightenment, coming late and in its more radical form, was action-directed and emotion-laden (for example, Kozel'sky's plea in 1767 for emancipation). The notions of the *Aufklärung* and of the French Enlightenment were infused with moral passion to provoke the first direct criticism and protest, as well as appeal to action, on the part of the Russian elite that had absorbed their message in the reign of Catherine II.

The first expressions of the Russian reaction to these ideas are to be found in *belles lettres,* especially in the satirical drama and

---

[2] Catherine II "pilfered" Montesquieu's *Esprit des Lois* for her Nakaz. But the choice is significant, since Montesquieu favored a liberal *Ständestaat*. Besides, copying Montesquieu does not mean understanding or fully accepting his ideas. In matters of social and economic policy, and also in the relevant paragraphs of the Nakaz, Catherine appears to have been more influenced by such cameralists as Justi and Bielefeldt.

О твердая моихъ надежда странъ едина.
Прими усердіе отъ всѣхъ, ЕКАТЕРИНА.
Пребудетъ въ вѣкъ ТЕБѢ опредѣленна части,
Судомъ и вѣрою украшенная власть.

Catherine the Great—typical allegorical representation

journalism of the last third of the eighteenth century. Satire was the preferred vehicle, for it combined entertainment and didacticism with a veiled and limited critique of moral reality. It was attractive to a society still in the process of formation, and it was deemed acceptable by a suspicious government. It was not overly radical and did not strike at the roots of the institutional framework, while it promoted proper values for obedient and responsible subjects. Even Catherine II joined in this literary game, although she stopped short of searching criticism of the most basic facets of Russian reality—for instance, serfdom.

*The satirist was freer in expressing his ideas and drawing social lessons from his observations. In attacking the obvious defects of Russian life, where he found himself in accord with Catherine's own satirical writings, he could put his positive message across quite openly. This approach was followed by the playwrights V. Kapnist (1757–1823) and D. I. Fonvizin, and more particularly by the great journalist N. I. Novikov (1744–1818). On a superficial level, like Catherine II, Fonvizin, and others, Novikov was directing his barbs at the fops and dandies who aped the externals of Western (especially French) manners and customs, yet remained semibarbarous moral beings. But on a deeper level, he was castigating the superficiality, irresponsibility, corruption, and even criminality of the Russian upper classes. The ridicule of their outward manners and dress bespoke an even worse inner condition, their moral emptiness and callousness. It was this moral deficiency that made them indifferent to the miseries of their fellow-men, the serfs. This indifference led them into accepting as normal criminal and brutal acts destructive of their own humanity, as well as that of their victims. Novikov advocated, therefore, a moral regeneration of the elite to turn their attention inward, to make them see their own spiritual shortcomings and their duty toward their fellow-men, especially defenseless peasants and domestics.

As education and enlightenment were the most effective means for success in such a program, Novikov became a leading publisher. Besides his satirical journals, he published children's magazines and popular scholarly reviews. To make more accessible to the average Russian the treasure trove of Western culture, Novikov organized the "Friendly Society for the Promotion of Translations," which made available in Russian all the literary and philosophical classics of Europe. To spread knowledge and ideas in the provinces, he organized local publishing houses, reading rooms, and lending libraries. He was most influential in bringing to a large audience beyond the confines of the capital the ideas of the *Aufklärung* and of the French Enlightenment, as well as the best works of Russia's young literature and scholarship. He paid much attention to Russia's historical heritage. To make it available and better known, he undertook the publication, in *Russkaia vivliofika*, of the major sources of Russia's history; together with Golikov, he helped to publish a vast amount of material on the reign of Peter the Great. He thus gave the Russian elite access to Russia's past, and prepared the climate in which the great history of Nicholas Karamzin found eager and responsive readers a quarter of a century later.*

Last, we should not forget the reaction to, and the lesson derived from, the Pugachev rebellion, although it is not easy to assess its full impact and nature. There can be no doubt that the revolt generated among the nobility neurotic fear of another bloody rising. This led to demands for more effective protection from the state and the insistence that any weakening of controls would most likely result in the destruction of the Russian state. But such an attitude was not typical of the educated elite, of those who were in the process of creating modern Russian culture and formulating its values. Some saw in the Russian peasant a child, basically good-natured, but given to occasional violent, destructive outbursts. As Karamzin (1766–1826), steeped in sentimentalism and maudlin Rousseauism, was at pains to show, the peasant not only had the same feelings as any human being; his feelings could be as noble and as beautiful as those of the nobleman. In addition, the serf was capable of the greatest devotion, self-abnegation, and courage. Karamzin succeeded superbly in putting his point across, for his stories not only helped to create a new Russian prose style, they also created a new image of the peasant as a human being of great emotional and moral worth.

But still, the serf was a child, and he had to be protected against himself, his rages, his outbursts of violence and destructiveness which could bring harm not only to others, but also to himself. Karamzin therefore advocated a benevolent paternalism, respectful of the peasant's childish emotions and good moral qualities, but careful not to give him a degree of freedom that was beyond his capacity. Kindness, benevolence—yes, but full freedom—no, since the best for both serf and master was fatherly control and guidance. This attitude toward the peasantry came to be shared by the majority of the serf-owning nobility in the early nineteenth century; it was related to the view of the emperor as the "super-father" who helped the individual landowner to exercise benevolent control over his serfs, while also seeing to it that no master abused his power over the peasants for evil. This is the political message of a benevolent and humane conservative autocracy based on serfdom, which Karamzin expounded as a truly Russian alternative to Speransky's rationalistic and liberal reforms inspired by irrelevant Western models (*Of Old and New Russia,* ca. 1812). Karamzin's ideas were a significant ingredient in later Slavophile theories, and they became the bible of moderately liberal conservatives throughout the nineteenth century, who after 1861–1864 transferred this image of the landlord to the zemstvo leadership.

But Karamzin's was not the only conclusion drawn from the experience of the Pugachev revolt. It also brought into sharp focus the full extent of the evil of serfdom, its dehumanizing and brutalizing effect on both master and serf. It revealed the shaky and flammable foundation on which the imperial system rested, since serfdom could provoke a destructive, pitiless upsurge such that it might be the undoing of the Russian polity. It was recognized that, since the serf was a moral and rational human being, his revolt against oppression was perfectly understandable and justified. The task of those who had become aware of the situation, of the cultural and educated elite, was therefore to take measures that would transform the system. This was best done by that same elite, whose notions of service and social responsibility should now be focused on the people. They had done their duty to the state; now they should lead in reforms to free the peasant, to give him scope for the full development of his moral, intellectual, and spiritual potential. In any event, the continuation of serfdom was contrary to all the moral principles held and expounded by the educated everywhere. It was contrary to civilization and humanity, and for that reason alone, could not be tolerated without serious danger to all of Russia.

This was the message that Alexander Radishchev (1749–1802) endeavored to spread; and he did so with a passionate commitment that bespoke the influence of Pietism, of the *Aufklärung,* as well as of the later *philosophes* (especially Raynal). Unfortunately, Radishchev had cried out, "I looked around me and my heart was filled with pity," and advocated a radical attack on the evil of serfdom at the wrong moment. He published his *Journey from St. Petersburg to Moscow,* containing this message, in 1790, when the French Revolution had frightened Catherine II. The empress not only forbade and destroyed Radishchev's book, but also had the author arrested, tried, and condemned to death—a sentence which she commuted to exile in Siberia. Paul I allowed Radishchev to return to St. Petersburg, and Alexander I made him a member of the Commission on Codification; but Radishchev could never again be as active as he wished, and he committed suicide in 1802. Radishchev's portrayal of the social and political consequences of the Pugachev revolt, his unqualified condemnation of serfdom and tyranny, as well as the inkling he had that change had to come through passionate commitment to action on the part of the elite—these were to be the intellectual and political guidelines of the emerging intelligentsia for whom he became the first martyr and hero.[3]

The members of the generation of educated Russians who reached maturity and entered an active service career in the last decade of the eighteenth and the very first years of the nineteenth centuries

---

[3] The significance of Radishchev as an independent thinker and seminal writer has been much overplayed in Soviet historiography. It is true, however, that he reflected with great talent the prevailing philosophical, social, religious, and literary interests. But little of what he wrote was known at the time; he was "rediscovered" only in the nineteenth century.

focused their attention on the practical aspects of Russia's social and political problems. Chastened, no doubt, by the repression to which Radishchev, Novikov, and others had fallen victim at the end of Catherine's reign, kept silent by Paul's restrictive censorship, they were careful to avoid dealing directly with the most sensitive issues, and expressed their ideas in didactic dissertations instead of passionate, moralistic tracts. In the first years of the reign of Alexander I, when censorship was relaxed and when reform and change were in the air, this younger generation could state their ideas rather fully (even if the original version did not always pass the censor, especially after 1808). Raised on the satirical literature of the late eighteenth century, they agreed that much of Russia's difficulties stemmed from the intellectual, spiritual, and moral inadequacies of the upper classes. Their first concern, therefore, was to develop an educational system that would adequately prepare the elites for their tasks as "true sons of the fatherland," while helping the lower classes, especially the merchants and townspeople (but in the long run the free peasants also) to join the leadership ranks.

This was the burden of Ivan Pnin's (1773–1805) best-known work, *An Essay on Enlightenment with Reference to Russia*. In it, Pnin goes back to Locke and the sensualistic-empirical psychology of the Franco-English Enlightenment, although he does not forget the precepts taught by Rousseau, especially with respect to the formation of a good heart and proper moral attitudes. What is interesting, however, and it clearly sets the limits of Pnin's reformism, is that he believed education should be a function of one's role in society, of one's station in life. Thus truly full education, with a special emphasis on the sense of moral responsibility, is to be restricted to the nobility; the middle classes are to be taught the basic economic skills, as well as the moral tenets of honesty and reliability that are expected from merchants. Only the mechanical arts, with a minimum of reading and writing, and a strong emphasis on religion were to constitute the education of the peasantry, although efforts were to be made to introduce them to better techniques and agricultural knowledge. In Pnin's scheme the reform of the education of the clergy would automatically bring forth priests who could play a significant part in raising the cultural as well as material level of the villages (the priest would set an example and minister to the body as well as to the soul).

Pnin's collaborator and friend, Alexander Bestuzhev (1761–1810), father of several future Decembrists, paid more attention to education in state-run boarding schools where future officers were to be trained. He too stressed the development of the proper moral sense and high-mindedness as essential qualities of the defender of the fatherland. In addition, he stressed a well-rounded and technically sophisticated general education for the future officer. Such broad knowledge was necessary not only for leadership in the army, but also for civilian duties such as those of an effective landlord.

Obviously, education was only the means for developing the kind of subject who would be most needed in a reformed Russian state. The significant element in the thought of Pnin and Bestuzhev, but even more so in that of their friend Vasilii Popugaev (ca. 1779–1816), who concentrated on political ideas, was that government, including the monarch, existed for a single purpose only: to promote and secure the welfare of the people. The system that had developed in Russia in the course of the eighteenth century was bad because it had perverted this original purpose and turned the state into an instrument for the promotion of the selfish interests of a small minority. The sovereign in turn had been deflected from his major role of fatherly protector and guide of the people into that of distributor of favors and shield for the malefactors among his courtiers. The emphasis was still on a transformation of the monarchical system that would bring out the basically good and moral qualities of the monarch as a means for meeting the people's needs. Popugaev and his friends barely discussed the institutional mechanisms that could bring about and preserve basic reforms. The people's happiness—the goal of society and of government—would be best secured by relying on the good will and purity of motive of the monarch, who would then know how to choose the best administrators. In short, the idea was to rely on good administrators rather than on good institutions (discretion and caution may have played a role in this formulation).

The young men further believed that the spiritual and intellectual level of the people would rise once the proper conditions for the nation's welfare had been secured and full freedom of action in the economic realm given to all Russians on an equal basis. Once this goal was reached, the common people could be drawn more into participating in administration. Significantly, monarchical leadership of the state and the ruler's initiative were not relinquished. Popugaev advocated a more humane, mild, welfare-oriented, benevolent absolutism. There is, however, Popugaev's recognition that with changes in the economy would come a transformation of society, which in turn would lead to reforms and adjustments in the political realm. To repeat, the state as a tool for the satisfaction of the base and material interests of a small minority must give way to a state that works for the welfare of the nation, under the moral leadership and personal supervision of the good monarch. The ethical and metaphysical underpinnings of this doctrine, as well as its extension to the realm of international policy, was the work of V. F. Malinovsky (1765–1814) in his *Discourse on Peace and War*.

These ideas were disseminated and elaborated thanks to the greater opportunities available for publishing and study in the first decade of the nineteenth century. The liberal censorship statute of 1804, as well as the government's dissemination of useful knowledge, led to the creation of new newspapers and journals, and heightened the activity in book publishing (which involved provincial centers as well). A special effort was made to bring to the Russian reading public contemporary Western ideas in economics, political economy, and technology, as well as the most recent discoveries and accomplishments of scholarship and science. Prominent among the new ideas that came to Russia were those of Adam Smith and Jeremy Bentham (whose brother served in the Russian administration); the organizational work of the Consulate and the Empire became widely known, as did disparate information on the United States, England, France, and Germany with respect to techniques and politics. Better information on the currents of ideas in the preceding century also became available, so that the Russian of 1820 was quite familiar with what went on (or had gone on previously) in the domains of philosophy, political ideas, political economy, and technology. In this respect, he was indistinguishable from any Western European of the same educational level. While not the most significant, the contribution of the French émigrés and the later refugees from the Napoleonic empire should not be forgotten as a source of information on new directions of European thought (Mme de Staël, J. De Maistre, Freihezz vom Stein, Ernst Moritz Arndt).

The character of the upper levels of the educational establishment was also undergoing a change. Although little was done to extend education to the majority of the people, the reign of Alexander I marks the beginning of the independent, scholarly role of the universities. In the first place, it was a matter of expanding facilities. To the single university of Moscow now were added those of Kharkov, Kazan, Dorpat (Iur'ev), and St. Petersburg. This was not all. Several new establishments of higher education, or at any rate schools offering general education on a high level with some specialization, were added (*lycées* at Iaroslavl', Nezhin, Odessa, Tsarskoe Selo, the Juridical Institute). Finally, a whole set of technical institutes, schools for crafts, as well as a greater number of secondary schools (*gymnasiia*), spread modern knowledge and scientific training to an ever-widening circle of the population. There was also the improved instruction given in the ecclesiastical schools following their reform in 1808. Not only did the quantity of university-level institutions rise sharply, but the quality of their instruction improved markedly. The professors active at the time belong to the first generation of Russian scholars; they set the standards that had to be met in preparing an ever-increasing number of professionals and scholars. In contrast to the eighteenth century, the numbers seemed great, but in absolute terms they were quite small, and the quality still left much to be desired. However, the first step had been taken, and a firm foundation was being laid.

The change is readily illustrated by the fact that most of the sons of the nobility in Moscow or Kazan were sent to attend the university; later the fashion spread to St. Petersburg, although never to the same extent (there were other special military schools and the *lycée* at Tsarskoe Selo available as alternatives). Many of these students from the nobility actually graduated with diplomas that gave them advanced standing in civilian service. We also begin to meet with sons of the upper nobility who are interested in scholarship not only as preparation for service, but for its own sake; although significantly, the notion that scholarly training could be of value in government service also begins to take hold. Quite a few students from the University of Moscow went abroad to perfect their knowledge, Göttingen being the most attractive center because of its reputation in political economy and history (and also because Professors Schlözer, father and son, were especially hospitable to young Russians). We thus find young Nicholas Turgenev writing a doctoral dissertation on serfdom, while his friend Andrei Kaisarov obtained his degree with a dissertation on Slavic folklore. Turgenev used his knowledge in government service to become a specialist in finance (*Essay on the Theory of Taxation*, 1818), while Kaisarov pursued an academic career, becoming professor of Slavic philology and literature at the University of Dorpat. It is not surprising, therefore, that their "younger brothers," when they came to Western Europe as officers in the armies in pursuit of Napoleon, also attended university lectures, acquainted themselves with the most recent scholarly literature in the fields that interested them (jurisprudence, political economy, political theory), and had much curiosity and not a little understanding about technology, agronomy, and the sciences.

Education and knowledge became fashionable and popular: Public lectures were a social event; they catered to the needs of those who could no longer attend schools or universities, as well as to ladies of good society who yearned to broaden their knowledge and come into contact with the dispensers of modern wisdom. The public lecture by scholars and writers became an important institution not only in spreading knowledge, but in enlivening the country's intellectual life and in stimulating open and wide discussion of new ideas.

The first decade of the nineteenth century proved seminal in the history of the Russian intelligentsia in still another respect: It witnessed the first *kruzhok*, an informal circle of close friends organized for the purpose of widening their mental and artistic horizons through reading and discussion of recent philosophical and esthetic currents.[4] The circle that formed around Andrei Turgenev, an older brother of Nicholas, in Moscow in 1801–1802 played the most important role in introducing German Romantic literature (especially Schiller) and philosophy (Kant and Fichte). One member of the circle, V. Zhukovsky, became the most influential early Romantic poet and major translator of German and English verse. This kind of "circle" arose out of its members' need to define their own identity. They felt they could not identify with their parents, whose life seemed hypocritical, since it wavered between the rhetoric of high-sounding morality and social responsibility on the one hand, and the cruel practice of serf ownership on the other. In their search for identity, they turned to their own peers, among whom they singled out as heroes those who seemed endowed with particularly remarkable qualities of moral purity, spiritual integrity, and intellectual receptivity. They also tried to forge an identity for themselves by seeking and discovering a more satisfying view of the world in contemporary foreign writing on philosophy and esthetics. Schiller was the inspiration in the circle of 1802, Schelling for the circle of *"liubomudry"* ("lovers of wisdom," "philosophers") around V. F. Odoevsky in the early 1820s in Moscow; Hegel played this role in the early 1830s. The new identity might also involve a new relationship between the members of the circle—the intelligentsia—and Russia (that is, the nation's history) and the people. Strong ties of friendship and intellectual harmony within the circles became the cement that was to give cohesion and shape to the Russian intelligentsia in the years to come.

The generation that was drawn into the struggle against Napoleon was therefore much more mature, and intellectually and spiritually more sophisticated, than any of its predecessors. The wars of 1812–

---

[4] There were some vague antecedents for this kind of circle, but they did not have its emotional impact, nor were they as original in their intellectual search. Among such predecessors we may mention the circle organized in the middle of the eighteenth century by the pupils of the Corps of Cadets to produce plays, translations, and a literary magazine. An informal group was also organized under Khersakov's sponsorship at the University of Moscow; and the director of the Boarding School for Nobles at the University of Moscow, Prokopovich-Antonsky, set up a formal literary society for the pupils (they also published an almanac and had regular readings of literary pieces, their own compositions or translations). But the *kruzhok* also differed from all previous organizations in that it was a strictly private undertaking.

1815 revealed to the members of this educated elite the heretofore unknown patriotism of the Russian people and served to intensify their own nationalism, to arouse in them the fervent desire to crown the liberation from the foreign invader with political and social reforms. They expected the tsar to reward his people for their patriotism and steadfastness by granting them freedom, while providing the elite with an opportunity to be useful. Those who went to Western Europe with the Russian armies, or who went later, also learned a great deal about the way in which economic, social, and political problems were handled there. Contacts with the intellectual and political elites of the West—for example, the German nationalist *Tugenbund*, the political salons of Paris—widened the scope of their knowledge and understanding of political ideas and practices. They returned home full of hope and bursting with eagerness to act on their ideas, beliefs, and experiences.

Nicholas Turgenev founded a society whose main function was the spread of civic education through the publication of a journal and the creation of a network among officials to assist them in the performance of their duties, to foster emulation, and to place the best men in key positions. General Fedor Orlov established an "Order of Russian Knights," a mixture of a Masonic lodge and a patriotic association *à la Tugenbund*, but it did not develop beyond the planning stage. Many officers devoted much of their time and effort to spreading education among their soldiers (for example, introducing the Lancasterian system of schools in the Southern Corps in the Ukraine). Some tried to improve their peasants' lot and even considered freeing their serfs. (They were usually prevented from doing so by their alarmed neighbors and local authorities.) They organized study circles and attended lectures; the most influential of the latter was the lecture series and the discussion circle of Professor A. P. Kunitsyn (1793–1840), author of a much-read treatise on natural law (1818). The book was essentially a restatement of the major beliefs and notions of the *Aufklärung* and of the Enlightenment, although in rather moderate tone and form. Kunitsyn stressed the necessity for a social organization that would maintain justice and the moral law, and protect the spiritual independence and freedom of every citizen.

Under Russian conditions, these efforts could not be carried on without the permission of and supervision by the state. But instead of finding a sympathetic reception for their reform plans, the liberal officers were confronted with Alexander's conservative mysticism and indifference, and with the brutal militarism and tyranny of the military colonies. Garrison life was deadening; the intellectual atmosphere increasingly stifling. Literature was no longer adequate to express and focus the energies of this post-Napoleonic generation. Besides the purely literary *Arzamas*, there were formed societies that had social concerns as well. Thus, for example, the Free Society of Lovers of Letters, Science, and Arts (*Vol'noe obshchestvo liubitelei slovesnosti, nauk i khudozhestv*) was involved in philanthropic activities. Among its prominent members were men who, through their official connections (F. Glinka, for instance, was on the staff of the influential military governor of the capital, General Miloradovich), hoped to bring about a sounder policy and to reorient the course of the government. In the final analysis, however, none of the activities we have mentioned and none of the societies we have listed satisfied the great urge for meaningful, constructive action to bring about basic transformations in Russian society and government.

Ironically, a literary work conservative in purpose poured fuel on the smoldering discontent. In 1818 Karamzin completed publication of his *History of the Russian State*. Politically, his was a perfectly loyalist and monarchist interpretation; even Ivan IV was praised for having kept the country together and parried the danger of a break-up of the state. Most important, it was eminently readable; it acquainted a large stratum of Russian society with the history of their country, which stood revealed for the first time in all its glory. But within the chronicle readers also discovered aspects of a freer past that they had not known, or only vaguely suspected. The history of the free republics of Novgorod and Pskov and their struggle for independence, the heroic resistance to the Mongols, and similar episodes inspired many young Russians with a sense of pride in the free past of their fatherland. The suspicious thought arose that perhaps the regime of the Romanovs, at least in its contemporary form, was not the "natural" outcome of a genuinely Russian historical development. A new sense of identity, anchored in a sense of mission to help the nation, strengthened by pride in the glorious deeds and the free past of their ancestors, was gradually taking hold of the most sensitive and progressive members of the nobility.

Disappointed in their efforts to contribute to the good of the country, and inspired by the conspiracies that had led to uprisings in Spain, Italy, Greece, and Latin America in the 1820s, the young men of the elite turned to organizing secret societies and conspiring against the Establishment. Eventually, three societies emerged from these secret goups: Northern, Southern, and United Slavs. They organized to discuss programs, tactics, and possibly prepare for a violent overthrow of the existing system. Seizing the opportunity offered by the confusion which accompanied the accession of Nicholas I in December 1825, they staged a coup in St. Petersburg and a mutiny in the Ukraine. The rising that took place in the capital on December 14, 1825, gave this group the name "Decembrists."

The history of the Decembrist movement is fairly well known (there is a vast literature), so that only a few highlights will be touched upon here. In point of fact, the Decembrists never made concrete plans and preparations for direct political action. Their coup in St. Petersburg failed not only because the government retained control of the artillery, but also because the Decembrists were not supported by society and because they did not know what to do once they had lined up their soldiers in front of the Senate building. Their failure to act, their lack of preparation for action, were as much the cause of their immediate defeat as the strength of the Establishment. One of the reasons for this failure was that they had not reached a consensus on a program—or even on the basic foundations of their political outlook. They were in agreement that serfdom had to be abolished, that the bureaucratic, militaristic regime of the emperor should be replaced by some system that would be more liberal, possibly even constitutional. But this was about as far as they had gone in their planning. As a matter of fact, since about 1821 there had been many defections from the Decembrist groups because of this failure to define their common principles and a joint program. Only the fortuitous events of December swelled their ranks with a number of officers friendly with the leaders of the Decembrist societies who happened to be around and who followed them into the coup and mutiny.

Two major orientations did become manifest among the so-called Northern and Southern societies (from their location in St. Petersburg and in the Ukraine). We may ignore the United Slavs, who finally merged with the Southern Society; their originality lay in advocacy of a federation of all Slavic peoples, including even the Magyars, whom they erroneously defined as Slavs. The Northern Society advocated a constitutional arrangement that was much influenced by the Constitution of the United States, with some federalism, limited suffrage, basic rights, and a very moderate conservative plan for the emancipation of the serfs and the improvement of the peasantry's lot. The document setting forth this orientation was the so-called Constitution of Nikita Muraviev, a leader in the Northern Society. The leadership of the Southern Society felt that only seizure of power, a temporary dictatorship, a far-reaching program of social and economic reforms, a centralized administration (possibly a republican one) could put Russia on the path to freedom and modernization. The advocate of this approach was Colonel Paul Pestel, leader of the Southern Society, whose draft constitution, "Russian Justice" ("*Russkaia pravda*"), reflected the energy and harshness of the Jacobins by whom he had been much influenced and whose single-mindedness, energy, hard-headed rationalism he shared. Pestel did depart from his French inspiration in one respect: he felt that the welfare of the Russian peasant would be best secured within the communal framework. The minimum amount of land required to guarantee their livelihood was to be owned by the commune in perpetuity, although the individual peasant could possess any additional land he acquired on his own. Pestel has often been called a Socialist; yet he thought of communal land ownership not as the foundation of the economic system, but rather as an insurance against bad times for the poorest peasant.

The revolt staged by the Northern Society on December 14 on Senate Square (and the mutiny of some small military units in the Ukraine which followed a few weeks later) failed. The formation of several battalions of the St. Petersburg garrison in front of the Senate was dispersed by artillery, and the leaders quickly rounded up. Nicholas I was in full control. The Decembrists were first interrogated at length (the record of their interrogations is our main source for the whole movement), then tried by a special court and convicted. Five were hanged; another one hundred and twenty drew sentences of prison, hard labor, and exile of varying lengths. Most of the sentences were mitigated in the 1830s and 1840s, and Alexander II eventually amnestied those who were still alive in the late 1850s. As almost all the Decembrists had connections with the best and most prominent Russian noble families, there was hardly a family at court or in the capital that did not have one of its members implicated in the movement. The failure of an obviously poorly prepared revolt led the upper classes to feel that the punishment had been too harsh, even if the intent had been quite subversive from the government's point of view.

The Decembrists' unquestionable idealism, selflessness, and dedication to the good of the fatherland made a profound impression on Russian society. Many Decembrists survived the first decade of their worst ordeal; eventually, they were allowed to settle in Siberia, and still later to return to Russia. They wrote their memoirs and made their case known—and in the process obviously stressed their hopes and ideals. Seen from this perspective, their martyrdom seemed that much greater (their wives' decision to follow them to Siberia added a sentimental and romantic touch to their fate). In short, Russian society (*obshchestvo*)—that is, the thinking and educated segment of the elite—felt that Nicholas had gone too far, that the punishment of the Decembrists was undeserved. "Society" felt this incident marked its parting of the ways with the Establishment (the government). The fate of the Decembrists made final the split between "us," the emerging intelligentsia and "society," and "they," the state. At the same time, the Decembrists gave birth to the tradition of the Russian revolutionary movement and provided its first martyr-heroes. In this sense, the Decembrist revolt and the accession of Nicholas I mark a divide in the history of imperial Russia.

Bibliography

The bibliography has been designed to assist the student and reader in going beyond the text of the present volume rather than to illustrate and bolster the author's interpretations. General histories which should be consulted for any aspect of the period and the main bibliographical tools for further research are listed in the first section; subsequent sections are arranged topically by chapter. The stress is on useful works in English, but the basic and classic monographs in Russian (and other Western languages) have been included as well. Throughout, preference has been given to those titles that are both most recent and most useful as further bibliographical guides.

1. Political Chronicle—General

The classical general histories of Russia cover at least some of the topics dealt with in this book, although their stress is on the earlier period: S. M. Soloviev, *Istoriia rossii s drevneishikh vremen*, 15 vols. (Moscow, 1959–66); V. O. Kliuchevsky, *"Kurs russkoi istorii,"* latest edition, vols. 1–5 of his *Sochineniia* (Moscow, 1956–58). An early English translation is not good, but the parts dealing with the seventeenth century and the reign of Peter the Great have been nicely retranslated recently: V. O. Kliuchevsky, *A Course in Russian History—The Seventeenth Century*, trans. Natalie Duddington, introd. Alfred Rieber (Chicago, 1968); and V. O. Kliuchevsky, *Peter the Great*, trans. and introd. Liliana Archibald (New York, 1961). S. F. Platonov, *Lektsii po russkoi istorii* (St. Petersburg, 1904); *Ocherki istorii SSSR*, 9 vols. (Moscow, 1953–58). The most recent Soviet general history is *Istoriia SSSR s drevneishikh vremen do nashikh dnei v dvukh seriiakh v dvenadtsati tomakh*, 1st series, vols. 1–6 (Moscow, 1966–68). The classic for the nineteenth century is

A. A. Kornilov, *Kurs istorii XIX veka*, 3 vols. (Petrograd, 1918), for which there is an English translation: A. A. Kornilov, *Modern Russian History from the Age of Catherine the Great to the End of the Nineteenth Century*, trans. A. S. Kaun, bibliog., J. S. Curtiss (New York, 1943). See also Kornilov, *Istoriia Rossii v XIX veka*, 9 vols. (St. Petersburg, 1907–11).

Of the general histories in Western European languages, only the following deserve mention here: K. Stählen, *Geschichte Russlands von den Anfängen bis zur Gegenwart*, 4 vols. (Berlin, 1923–39); P. Miliukov, C. Seignobos, L. Eisenmann, *Histoire de la Russie*, 3 vols. (Paris, 1935), also available in English translation by C. L. Markmann, 3 vols. (New York, 1968); Hugh Seton-Watson, *The Russian Empire 1801–1917* (Oxford, 1967).

The general bibliographies of Russian history in English are very unsatisfactory, although they may be useful for beginning students: D. Shapiro, *A Select Bibliography of Works in English on Russian History, 1801–1917* (Oxford, 1962); C. Morley, *Guide to Research in Russian History* (Syracuse University, 1951); P. L. Horecky, ed., *Basic Russian Publications: An Annotated Bibliography on Russia and the Soviet Union* (University of Chicago, 1962). In spite of its somewhat specialized focus, the section on Russia D/9 by Marc Szeftel in John Gilissen, ed., *Bibliographical Introduction to Legal History and Ethnology* (Etudes d'Histoire et d'Ethnologie juridiques, Université Libre de Bruxelles, 1966) is a valuable and reliable guide to the literature and sources on institutional history. For the growing number of doctoral dissertations in the field of Russian history, consult J. J. Dossick, *Doctoral Research on Russia and the Soviet Union* (New York University, 1960). See also the follow-up article in *Slavic Review*, XXIII (December 1964), 797–812; an updated edition has been promised. Dissertations defended in France and Germany are listed in the major Slavic periodicals of these countries. For the very complicated problem of Soviet dissertations, see Eleanor Buist, "Soviet Dissertation Lists since 1934," *The Library Quarterly*, XXXIII, 2 (April 1963), 192–207.

The following Soviet bibliographical collections are essential for any research in Russian history, despite their selectivity: E. M. Zhukov, ed., *Sovetskaia Istoricheskaia Entsiklopediia*, 14 vols., of which 12 have appeared (Moscow, 1961————); *Istoriia SSSR: Annotirovannyi perechen' russkikh bibliografii, izdannykh do 1965 g.*, 2nd ed. (Moscow, 1966); *Istoriia SSSR: Ukazatel' sovetskoi literatury za 1917–1952 gg.*, 2 vols., plus 2 index vols. (Moscow, 1956–58). In addition, the comprehensive bibliographies on the history of Russian literature are of great assistance: V. P. Stepanov, Iu. V. Stennik, and P. N. Berkov, eds., *Istoriia russkoi literatury XVIII veka: Bibliograficheskii ukazatel'* (Leningrad, 1968); K. D. Muratova, *Istoriia russkoi literatury XIX veka: Bibliograficheskii ukazatel'* (Moscow-Leningrad, 1962). For a guide to primary sources and their publication, see M. N. Tikhomirov, *Istochnikovedenie istorii SSSR,* 2 vols. (Moscow, 1940; 2nd ed., vol. 1 only, Moscow, 1962); S. N. Valk, *Sovetskaia arkheografiia* (Moscow, 1948). For biographical data, the surest guide is the comprehensive bibliography of I. M. Kaufman, *Russkie biograficheskie i biobibliograficheskie slovari* (Moscow, 1955).

An easy selective guide to periodicals is *Russkaia periodicheskaia pechat'* (1702–1894): spravochnik (Moscow, 1959), 1895–October 1917 (Moscow, 1957); and N. Smirnov-Sokol'sky, *Russkie literaturnye al'manakhi i sborniki XVIII–XIX vv* (Moscow, 1965).

For German-language articles in periodicals, there are two handy and comprehensive guides: Klaus Meyer, *Bibliographie der Arbeiten zur osteuropäischen Geschichte aus den deutschsprachigen Fachzeitschriften 1858–1964,* Hrgb. W. Philipp (Bibliographische Mitteilungen des Osteuropa Instituts an der Freien Universität Berlin, Heft 9, 1966); Klaus-Dieter Seemann and Frank Siegmann, *Bibliographie der slavistischen Arbeiten aus den deutschsprachigen Fachzeitschriften 1876–1963* (Bibliographische Mitteilungen des Osteuropa Instituts an der Freien Universität Berlin, Heft 8, 1965).

The most important serials in the field of Russian history currently being published are: *Slavic Review* (formerly *American Slavic and East European Review*), *Canadian Slavic Studies* (Montreal), *Slavonic and East European Review* (London), *Jahrbücher für Geschichte Osteuropas* (Munich), *Forschungen zur osteuropäischen Geschichte* (Freie Universität, Berlin), *Oxford Slavonic Papers* (England), *Cahiers du monde russe et soviétique* (Paris). The two Soviet periodicals are *Voprosy istorii* and *Istoriia SSSR.* The prerevolutionary periodicals primarily concerned with history were *Russkaia Starina, Russkii Arkhiv,* and *Istoricheskii Vestnik.* After 1917, there were also important materials published in *Krasnyi Arkhiv, Istoricheskie Zapiski,* and *Istoricheskii Arkhiv.*

The principal collections of sources for the imperial period are: *Polnoe sobranie zakonov rossiiskoi imperii* (St. Petersburg, 1830–39; 1st series, 1649–1825); *Sbornik imperatorskogo russkogo istoricheskogo obshchestva,* 148 vols. (St. Petersburg, 1867–1916); *Chteniia v Imperatorskom obshchestve istorii i drevnostei rossiikikh,* 264 vols. (Moscow, 1846–1918).

2. The Empire

Outside of the old nineteenth-century histories of regiments and military campaigns, the historiography of the Russian army and navy is very meager. The best introduction, however, is provided by volumes published or edited by the Soviet military historian L. G. Beskrovnyi: his *Ocherki voennoi istoriografii Rossii* (Moscow, 1962) are an invaluable introduction to both sources and monographs. The *Russkaia voennaia periodicheskaia pechat' (1702–1916): Bibliograficheskii ukazatel'* (Moscow, 1959) provides the necessary guide to serials. For the first half of the period covered in this volume, there is a comprehensive and informative monograph, L. G. Beskrovnyi, *Russkaia armiia i flot v XVIII veke (Ocherki)* (Moscow, 1958); many specific aspects and details are illuminated in the collective volume, *Voprosy voennoi istorii Rossii (XVIII i pervaia polovina XIX vekov)* (Moscow, 1969), honoring Beskrovnyi.

Russia's foreign policy may be best studied in the general histories of European diplomacy in the eighteenth and nineteenth centuries. A useful bibliographical introduction is found in the otherwise not very satisfactory monograph by P. K. Grimsted, *The Foreign Ministers of Alexander I (Political Attitudes and the Conduct of Russian Diplomacy, 1801–1825)* (University of California, 1969). There is little on the formation of the Russian Empire; the only attempt at a comprehensive analysis (mainly in institutional and juridical terms), with a valuable bibliography, is B. Nolde, *La formation de l'empire russe: études, notes, documents*, 2 vols. (Paris, 1952–53). The juridical aspects of the nature of the empire have been brilliantly analyzed by Baron B. E. Nol'de, "Edinstvo i nerazdel'nost' rossii," in his *Ocherki russkogo gosudarstvennogo prava* (St. Petersburg, 1911), pp. 223–554.

The China trade and its consequences are described by C. M. Foust, *Muscovite and Mandarin: Russia's Trade with China and Its Setting, 1727–1805* (University of North Carolina, 1969).

The conquest of the Baltic provinces, as well as the diplomatic and military events of Peter's reign, is well described by R. Wittram, *Peter I, Czar und Kaiser (Peter der Grosse in Seiner Zeit)*, 2 vols. (Göttingen, 1964). The subsequent evolution of the relations between these provinces and the Russian state are dealt with from a biographical point of view by Wittram in *Drei Generationen: Deutschland, Livland, Russland* (Göttingen, 1949), while the socio-institutional aspects are comprehensively covered by Ia. Zutis, *Ostzeiskii vopros v XVIII veke* (Riga, 1946). Some interesting remarks of a more theoretical character may be found in G. von Rauch, *Russland: Staatliche Einheit und nationale Vielfalt* (Munich, 1953). On the incorporation of Finland and its subsequent history, see P. Scheibert, "Die Anfänge der finnischen Staatswerdung unter Alexander I," *Jahrbücher für Geschichte Osteuropas*, IV, 3–4 (1939). M. G. Schybergson, *Politische Geschichte Finlands, 1809–1919)* (Stuttgart, 1925).

For the complicated history of Poland, the best starting point is *The Cambridge History of Poland,* 2 vols. (Cambridge, Eng., 1950–51). On Byelorussia, there is a revealing collection of documents: *Belorussiia v epokhu feodalizma,* vols. 2 and 3 (Minsk, 1960–61). The history of the Jews under Russian rule is summarized reliably, although in an old-fashioned manner, by S. M. Dubnow, *History of the Jews in Russia and Poland from the Earliest Times Until the Present Day,* 3 vols. (Philadelphia, 1916, reprinted 1946). The history of the Ukraine is still a much-neglected field. The classical nationalistic, but moderate, point of view is that of M. Hrushevsky, *A History of the Ukraine* (Yale University, 1941); this is a condensation of the multivolume work in Ukrainian. A good English summary is in W. E. D. Allen, *The Ukraine: A History* (Cambridge, Eng., 1940). The official Soviet viewpoint is stated in *Istoriia Ukrainskoi SSR,* 2 vols. (Kiev, 1956), while the social trends following the incorporation of the Ukraine into the Russian state are nicely dealt with by V. A. Miakotin, *Ocherki sotsial'noi istorii Ukrainy XVII–XVIII vv,* 3 vols. (Prague, 1926). The settlement of the Ukraine by foreign and Russian settlers is described in great detail by N. D. Polons'ka-Vasylenko, *The Settlement of the Southern Ukraine, The Annals of the Ukrainian Academy of Arts and Sciences in the U.S.,* vols. IV–V (Summer–Fall 1955), and more sweepingly in the posthumous monograph of H. Auerbach, *Die Besiedelung der Südukraine in den Jahren 1774–1787* (Wiesbaden, 1965), which also has an extensive and useful bibliography.

The history and problems involved in the relationship between the Cossack hosts and the imperial government have been dealt with in detail by S. G. Svatikov, *Rossiia i Don, 1549–1917* (Belgrade, 1924), and in the two volumes of V. A. Golobutsky, *Zaporozhskoe kazachestvo* (Kiev, 1957) and *Chernomorskoe kazachestvo* (Kiev, 1956). The former reflects a liberal and the latter a Soviet point of view. In addition, the incorporation of the northern shore of the Black Sea is described by E. I. Druzhinina in *Severnoe prichernomor'e v 1775–1800 gg* (Moscow, 1959), which stresses social and economic developments. The condition of the Crimea on the eve of its annexation by Russia and its incorporation are dealt with by A. W. Fisher, "The Russian Annexation of the Crimea, 1774–1783," in a dissertation defended at Columbia University in 1967 and due to be published in 1970 by Cambridge University Press. I have tried to give a synthesized discussion of Russian imperial policy in the eighteenth century in an article entitled "The Style of Russia's Imperial Policy and Prince G. A. Potemkin," in G. N. Grob, ed., *Statesmen and Statecraft of the Modern West* (Barre, Mass., 1967), pp. 1–51. The expansion into the steppes beyond the Volga has been described superficially by A. S. Donnelly, *The Russian Conquest of Bashkiria 1552–1740, A Case Study in Imperialism* (Yale University, 1968).

On Siberia, a brief sketch of its treatment by the imperial government, the nature of the reforms of Speransky, and bibliographical guidance may be found in M. Raeff, *Siberia and the Reforms of 1822* (Seattle, 1956). For a valuable treatment of the peasant settlement of the subcontinent (bringing the story down to the first years of the twentieth century), see Fr.-X. Coquin, *La Sibérie, Peuplement et immigration paysanne au XIXᵉ siècle* (Paris, 1969). Much useful information may be gleaned from *Istoriia Sibiri s drevneishikh vremen do nashikh dnei v piati tomakh* (Leningrad, 1968–69).

3. The Government

The basic source for the imperial government is the full collection of laws, *Polnoe sobranie zakonov,* 1st series, compiled in 1830. A descriptive handbook of the major institutions and their heads was compiled by Erik Amburger, *Geschichte der Behördenorganisation Russlands von Peter dem Grossen bis 1917* (Studien zur Geschichte Osteuropas, X, Leiden, 1966). A more complete repertory limited to the eighteenth century was compiled by A. V. Chernov, *Gosudarstvennye uchrezhdeniia Rossii v XVIII veka (Zakonodatel'nye materialy): Spravochnoe posobie* (Moscow, 1960).

Useful selections of major legislative acts for study purposes may be found in *Pamiatniki russkogo prava,* vol. 8, *Zakonodatel'nye akty Petra I* (Moscow, 1961), and in M. T. Beliavsky, ed., *Dvorianskaia imperiia XVIII veka (Osnovnye zakonodatel'nye akty): Sbornik dokumentov* (Moscow, 1960). Plans for reform, with a general interpretive discussion of the nature of the central government of the empire, are given in translation and excerpts in M. Raeff, *Plans for Political Reform in Imperial Russia, 1730–1905* (Englewood Cliffs, N.J., 1966).

The history of the imperial governmental institutions is best followed in the handbooks of Russian public law. The most influential of these is N. M. Korkunov, *Russkoe gosudarstvennoe pravo,* 2 vols., 5th ed. (St. Petersburg, 1905). A convenient short summary is provided by G. V. Vernadsky, *Ocherk istorii prava Russkogo gosudarstva XVIII–XIX vv (Period imperii)* (Prague, 1924). A recent Soviet handbook is N. P. Eroshkin, *Istoriia gosudarstvennykh uchrezhdenii dorevoliutsionnoi Rossii* (Moscow, 1968). Many facets are interestingly illuminated in the collective volume *Absoliutizm v Rossii (XVII–XVIII vv), Sbornik statei k semidesiatiletiiu so dnia rozhdeniia i sorokapiatiletiiu nauchnoi i pedagogicheskoi deiatel'-nosti B. B. Kafengauza* (Moscow, 1964).

For the reforms of Peter the Great, the handiest summary is Wittram, *op. cit.* Readable and intelligent summaries are provided by Wittram himself in *Peter der Grosse, Der Eintritt Russlands in die Neuzeit* (Berlin-Göttingen-Heidelberg, 1954), and in English by B. H. Sumner, *Peter the Great and the Emergence of Russia* (London, 1950). Excerpts from selected influential monographs and sources may be found in M. Raeff, *Peter the Great—Reformer or Revolutionary?* (Boston, 1963).

The problems of central supervision and coordination are analyzed in the old but still classic monograph of A. D. Gradovsky, "Vysshaia administratsiia Rossii XVIII st. i general prokurory," in his *Sochineniia,* vol. 1 (St. Petersburg, 1899), pp. 37–297. Local government is treated by M. M. Bogoslovsky, *Oblastnaia reforma Petra Velikogo: Provintsiia 1719–1727* (Moscow, 1902), and followed up by Iu. V. Got'e *Istoriia oblastnogo upravleniia ot Petra I do Ekateriny II,* 2 vols. (Moscow, 1913 and 1941). The government of Anna is discussed by V. Stroev, *Bironovshchina i Kabinet Ministrov (St. Petersburg,* 1909–10), and evaluated more positively than had been traditional by W. Slany, "Russian Central Government and Institutions, 1725–1741" (unpublished doctoral dissertation, Cornell University, 1958). An attempt at a reexamination of the reign of Peter III and some of the dynamic trends in mid-eighteenth century will be found in M. Raeff, "The Domestic Policies of Peter III and his Overthrow," to appear in the *American Historical Review* in June 1970. There still is no satisfactory history of the policies of Catherine II. Some light is shed in the important, but all too frequently ignored, monograph on Paul I: M. V. Klochkov, *Ocherki pravitel'stvuiushchei deiatel'nosti vremeni Pavla I* (Petrograd, 1916), some of whose interpretations are further developed by Claus Scharf, "Staatsauffassung und Regierungsprogramm eines aufgeklärten Selbstherrschers: Die Instruktion des Grossfürsten Paul von 1788," in E. Schulin, ed., *Gedenkschrift Martin Göhring: Studien zur europäischen Geschichte* (Wiesbaden, 1968), pp. 91–106. A significant contribution to the question of policy and court factions may be found in the unpublished doctoral dissertation by D. L. Ransel, "Nikita Panin's Role in Russian Court Politics of the Seventeen-sixties: A Critique of the Gentry Opposition Thesis" (Yale University, 1968). On a superficial level, there is useful information in P. Dukes, *Catherine the Great and the Russian Nobility* (Cambridge, Eng., 1967).

For the reforms of the reign of Alexander I, the easiest introduction is the study of M. Speransky: M. Raeff, *M. M. Speransky, States-*

man of Imperial Russia, 2nd ed. (The Hague, 1969), with bibliographies. The formation of Alexander's personal regime is described in a stimulating article by Allen McConnell, "Alexander I's Hundred Days: The Politics of a Paternalist Reformer," *Slavic Review* (December 1969) pp. 373–393. A Soviet interpretation is to be found in A. V. Predtechensky, *Ocherki obshchestvenno-politicheskoi istorii Rossii v pervoi chetverti XIX veka* (Moscow-Leningrad, 1957). A suggestive analysis of the bureaucracy is made by H. J. Torke, "Das russische Beamtentum in der ersten Hälfte des 19 Jahrhunderts," in *Forschungen zur osteuropäischen Geschichte,* vol. 13; the educational aspects are analyzed in the unpublished doctoral dissertation of J. T. Flynn, "The Universities in the Russia of Alexander I" (Clark University, 1964).

4. The Economy

Population statistics are found in V. E. Den, *Naselenie Rossii popiatoi revizii: Podushnaia podai' v XVIII v i statistika naseleniia v kontse XVIII v* (Moscow, 1902), and V. M. Kabuzan, *Narodonaselenie Rossii v XVIII—pervoi polovine XIX v (po materialam revizii)* (Moscow, 1963). The standard survey of Russian economic history is P. I. Liashchenko, *Istoriia narodnogo khoziaistva SSSR,* 2 vols. (Moscow, 1947–48), also available in English translation. The following multivolume survey of Russian economic thought also has useful information on the development of the country's economy: A. I. Pashkov, ed., *Istoriia russkoi ekonomicheskoi mysli,* 3 vols. of 5 (Moscow, 1955–66); the first volume is also available in English.

The economic policies of Peter the Great are analyzed in detail by P. N. Miliukov, *Gosudarstvennoe khoziaistvo Rossii v pervoi chetverti XVIII stoletiia i reforma Petra Velikogo,* 2nd ed. (St. Petersburg, 1905), which emphasizes the heavy cost of the Petrine reforms. The counterargument that the economic cost was not intolerable and permitted subsequent development was presented by B. B. Kafengauz, *Ocherki vnutrennogo rynka rossii pervoi poloviny XVIII veka (Po materialam vnutrennykh tamozhen)* (Moscow, 1958). A good summary of the policies and ideologies behind Peter's economic measures is the article by S. Blanc, "La politique économique de Pierre le Grand," *Cahiers du Monde russe et soviétique,* III (Janvier–Mars 1962).

For the industrialization of Russia in the reign of Peter I and later, see the general history of M. Tugan-Baranovsky, *Russkaia fabrika v proshlom i nastoiashchem,* 7th ed., vol. I (Moscow, 1938), and the history of the College of Manufactures, Dm. Baburin, *Ocherki po istorii Manufaktur Kollegii* (Moscow, 1939). The controversial question of Russian economic modernization is discussed by A. Kahan, "Continuity in Economic Activity and Policy During the Post-Petrine Period in Russia," *Journal of Economic History*, XXV (1965), 61–85. For the history of Russian trade, see I. M. Kulisher, *Istoriia russkoi torgovli do deviatnadtstogo veka vkliuchitel'no*, Peterburg 1923); for more specific aspects of the change in trade patterns and the relations with England, see D. Gerhard, *England und der Aufstieg Russlands* (Munich-Berlin, 1933).

The development of mining and heavy industry is discussed in a series of essays by P. Liubomirov, *Ocherki po istorii russkoi promyshlennosti* (Moscow, 1947), and with specific reference to the Ural industrial region, by R. Portal, *L'Oural au XVIIIe siècle* (Paris, 1950). The fate of the iron industry is ably traced by N. I. Pavlenko, *Istoriia metallurgii v rossii XVIII veka* (Moscow, 1962).

The literature on the peasant and serf question is immense; it is enough to mention first the general introduction by J. Blum, *Lord and Peasant in Russia from the Ninth to the Nineteenth Century* (Princeton University, 1961). The classic monograph on the peasants in the second half of the eighteenth century is V. Semevsky, *Krest'iane v tsarstvovanie imperatritsy Ekateriny II*, 2 vols. (St. Petersburg, 1881 and 1901). For an analysis of the social and psychological dimensions, see the stimulating monograph by M. Confino, *Domaines et seigneurs en Russie vers la fin du 18e siècle* (Paris, 1963). The specific problems and attitudes on economic matters of the nobility are discussed by W. R. Augustine, "The Economic Attitudes and Opinions Expressed by the Russian Nobility in the Great Commission of 1767" (unpublished doctoral dissertation, Columbia University, 1969). A general survey of the recent literature by M. Laran, "Nobles et paysans en Russie de l'âge d'or du servage à son abolition," *Annales Economies, Sociétés, Civilisations*, XXI, 1 (Janvier–Février, 1966). For the first half of the nineteenth century, an interesting economic microanalysis was made by I. D. Koval'chenko, *Russkoe krepostnoe krest'ianstvo v pervoi polovine XIX v* (Moscow, 1967). For the industrial, commercial, and technological development of the early nineteenth century, consult W. L. Blackwell, *The Beginnings of Russian Industrialization 1800–1860* (Princeton University, 1968).

The Soviet interpretation of Russian agriculture in the late eighteenth century is the important monograph by N. L. Rubinshtein, *Sel'skoe khoziaistvo vo vtoroi polovine XVIII v* (Moscow, 1957).

Public finance and questions connected with it are ably discussed by S. M. Troitsky, *Finansovaia politika russkogo absoliutizma v XVIII veke* (Moscow, 1966).

5. Social Classes

The legal position of the nobility has been described on the basis of all existing legislation by A. Romanovich-Slavatinsky, *Dvorianstvo v Rossii ot nachala XVIII veka do otmeny krepostnogo prava,* 2nd ed. (Kiev, 1912), while its corporate character and institutional role after 1762 has been analyzed by S. A. Korf, *Dvorianstvo i ego soslovnoe upravlenie za stoletie 1762–1855* (St. Petersburg, 1906). The social and cultural implications of state service are discussed in M. Raeff, *Origins of the Russian Intelligentsia: The 18th Century Nobility* (New York, 1966). The general economic and institutional aspects of the noble-serf relationship are discussed by P. Dukes, M. Confino, and W. R. Augustine, *op. cit.*

The peasant question in its economic and ideological dimensions is treated exhaustively in the monographs of P. K. Alefirenko, *Krest'ianskoe dvizhenie i krest'ianskii vopros v Rossii v 30–50kh godakh XVIII veka* (Moscow, 1958), and M. T. Beliavsky, *Krest'ianskii vopros v Rossii nakanune vosstaniia E. I. Pugacheva (Formirovanie antikrepostnicheskoi mysli)* (Moscow, 1965).

The historiography and events of the Pugachev rebellion are fully covered in the three-volume work edited by V. V. Mavrodin, of which the first two volumes have already appeared: *Krest'ianskaia voina v rossii 1773–1775 godakh: Vosstanie Pugacheva* (Leningrad, 1961–66). An attempt at analyzing the causes and character of the Pugachev revolt is to be found in the article by M. Raeff, "The Pugachev Rebellion—*Pugachevshchina,*" to be published in a volume dealing with revolutions in early modern history by the Johns Hopkins University Press, 1970). J. T. Alexander, *Autocratic Politics in a National Crisis: The Imperial Russian Government and Pugachev's Revolt 1773–1775* (Indiana University, 1969) summarizes the responses of the imperial administration to the peasant rebellion. A stimulating description of the changed image of the peasant in Russian literature following the revolt has been made by J.-L. Van Regemorter, "Deux images idéales de la paysannerie russe à la fin du XVIIIe siècle," *Cahiers du Monde russe et soviétique,* IX, 1 (1968), 5–19.

Discussions of the serf problem and plans to improve the peasants' lot are exhaustively summarized by V. I. Semevsky, *Krest'ianskii vopros v Rossii v XVIII i pervoi polovine XIX veka* (St. Petersburg, 1888). Some of the more practical measures taken in preparation for the general reform of the state peasantry in the reign of Nicholas I are thoroughly and intelligently discussed in N. M. Druzhinin, *Gosudarstvennye krest'iane i reforma P. D. Kiseleva,* 2 vols. (Moscow-Leningrad, 1946–58). On the military colonies, see R. Pipes, "The

Russian Military Colonies, 1810–1831," *Journal of Modern History*, XXII, 3 (September 1950), and the unpublished doctoral dissertation by A. D. Ferguson, "The Russian Military Settlements, 1810–1866" (Yale University, 1954). Much interesting and critical information is also to be found in the biography of Count A. A. Arakcheev by K. R. Whiting, "Aleksei Andreevich Arakcheev" (unpublished doctoral dissertation, Harvard University, 1951).

There is very little on the townspeople in the eighteenth and early nineteenth centuries. A. A. Kizevetter, *Posadskaia obshchina v Rossii XVIII st.* (Moscow, 1903) is the standard and exhaustive monograph. For the early nineteenth century, the book by the Soviet scholar P. G. Ryndziunsky, *Gorodskoe grazhdanstvo doreformennoi Rossii* (Moscow, 1958), is very informative. The book by V. Bill, *The Forgotten Class: The Russian Bourgeoisie from the Earliest Beginnings to 1900* (New York, 1959), hardly qualifies for serious consideration.

6. Church and Religion

The general history of the Eastern Church also has chapters dealing with Russia in the period under consideration: A. M. Ammann, *Abriss der ostslawischen Kirchengeschichte* (Vienna, 1950); an Italian version also exists. The following topically arranged study of the Russian Church and its clergy is of great value: I. Smolitsch, *Geschichte der russischen Kirche 1700–1917* (Studien zur osteuropäischen Geschichte, IX, Leiden, 1964). An erudite and original interpretation that stresses the positive side of the Synodal arrangement is A. V. Kartashev, *Ocherki po istorii russkoi tserkvi*, 2 vols. (Paris, 1959); the second volume covers the period 1700–1800.

Useful sources, with very suggestive introductions, are to be found in G. P. Fedotov, *A Treasury of Russian Spirituality* (New York, 1948). For the religious revival of the late eighteenth and early nineteenth centuries, see A. N. Pypin, *Religioznye dvizheniia pri Aleksandre I* (Petrograd, 1916). The specific problem of the Protestant and mystical influence, as well as its political dimensions, is ably discussed by J. C. Zacek, "The Russian Bible Society" (unpublished doctoral dissertation, Columbia University, 1964). The situation of the clergy and its education on the eve of the nineteenth century is briefly summarized (with bibliographical suggestions) by M. Raeff, *M. M. Speransky, op. cit.*

On the dissenters and Old Believers in the eighteenth and early nineteenth centuries, there is little literature. For the best introduction, besides the histories of the Church mentioned above, see P. N. Miliukov, *Ocherki istorii russkoi kul'tury*, vol. 2, part 1 (Paris, 1937);

it is also available in an edited English translation. See also the Soviet interpretation in A. I. Klibanov, *Istoriia religioznogo sektantstva v rossii* (Moscow, 1965). A recent work gives a full and fascinating picture of an important Old Believer community in our period: R. O. Krummey, *The Old Believers and the World of Antichrist—The Vyg Community and the Russian State 1694–1855* (Wisconsin, 1970). On the situation of the Catholics in the empire and their relationship to the government (with copious bibliography), see A. A. Brumanis, *Aux origines de la hiérarchie latine en Russie, Mgr Stanislas Siestrzencewicz-Bohusz, Premier archevêque-métropolitain de Mohilev 1731–1826* (Louvain, 1968). A revealing case study of a conversion to Catholicism is given by M. J. Rouet du Journel, *Une russe catholique: La vie de Madame Swetchine, 1782–1857* (Paris, 1953).

Related to the problem of the clergy is the origin and nature of the class of *raznochintsy*, intelligently discussed by C. Becker, "Raznochintsy: The Development of the Word and of the Concept," *American Slavic and East European Review*, XVIII, 1 (February 1959).

7. Education and Intellectual Life

Cultural and intellectual aspects of eighteenth-century history are treated by N. Miliukov, *Ocherki po istorii russkoi kul'tury*, vol. III (Paris, 1937), and Hans Rogger, *National Consciousness in 18th Century Russia* (Harvard University, 1960). An interesting although simple-minded and outdated Marxist approach is to be found in G. P. Plekhanov's *Istoriia russkoi obshchestvennoi mysli*, 3 vols. (Moscow, 1918. A useful survey was recently provided by H. Jablonowski, "Die geistige Bewegung in Russland in der 2 Hälfte des 18 Jahrhunderts," in Commission internationale des études slaves, *Ricerche Slavistiche* (Uppsala, 1960). The last chapter of Raeff, *Origins of the Russian Intelligentsia*, also touches on several important aspects and provides bibliographical suggestions.

A fair sample of eighteenth-century Russian writing is now available in translation in anthologies. The most comprehensive is that of H. B. Segel, *The Literature of Eighteenth-century Russia: A History and Anthology*, 2 vols. (New York, 1967). The first volume of the anthology *Russian Philosophy*, edited by J. M. Edie, J. P. Scanlan, and M. B. Zeldin (Chicago, 1965), contains excerpts from the writings of Skovoroda and Radishchev. The anthology edited by M. Raeff, *Russian Intellectual History, An Anthology* (New York 1966), contains representative writings on social and political problems. The standard histories of Russian literature by Mirsky, Slonim, and Blagoy (the latter on eighteenth-century literature specifically) should be consulted for general orientation. A useful guide to the Russian literature on the subject is provided by P. N. Berkov, *Vvedenie v izuchenie istorii russkoi literatury XVIII veka*, Part I, *Ocherk literaturnoi istoriografii XVIII veka* (Leningrad, 1964).

There is nothing in English on Pososhkov, Prokopovich, or Tatishchev that need be noted in the present context. A readable but not very original or overly reliable study on Tatishchev exists in German: C. Grau, *Der Wirtsschaftsorganisator, Staatsmann und Wissenschaftler Vasilij N. Tatiscev 1686–1750* (Berlin, 1963). The standard older biography of Lomonosov is B. N. Menshutkin, *Mikhailo Vasilievich Lomonosov—zhizneopisanie* (n.pl., 1911); which has been translated into English. Shcherbatov has had a revival of interest in recent years. His famous pamphlet, *On the Corruption of Morals in Russia*, has been translated with an introduction by A. Lentin (Cambridge University, 1969). A handy, albeit superficial, Soviet biography and interpretation is I. A. Fedosov, *Iz istorii russkoi obshchestvennoi mysli XVIII stoletiia—M. M. Shcherbatov* (Moscow, 1967). A different approach in evaluating Shcherbatov's thought in terms of the impact of the Petrine reforms has been attempted in M. Raeff, "State and Nobility in the Ideology of Prince M. M. Shcherbatov," *American Slavic and East European Review* (October 1960). On the important aspect of historical scholarship and writing, one should turn to the histories of Russian historiography. Unfortunately, there are none worthy of the name in English. For the best guidance, see N. L. Rubinshtein, *Russkaia istoriografiia* (Moscow, 1941), or the more detailed S. L. Peshtich, *Russkaia istoriografiia XVIII veka*, 2 vols. (Leningrad, 1961–65). The most stimulating treatment remains P. N. Miliukov, *Glavnye techeniia russkoi istoricheskoi mysli*, vol. I (Moscow, 1898).

On Russian educational institutions and the development of academic and technical training, there are only rather unsatisfactory books in English. The most comprehensive, although not fully reliable and quite superficial, is Alexander Vucinich, *Science in Russian Culture—A History to 1860* (Stanford University, 1963); it has a useful bibliography, however. The classic Russian monograph is S. Rozhdestvensky, *Ocherki po istorii sistem narodnogo prosveshcheniia v Rossii v XVIII–XIX vv* (St. Petersburg, 1912). Selected aspects have also been comprehensively dealt with in J. T. Flynn, "The Universities in the Russia of Alexander I" (unpublished doctoral dissertation, Clark University, 1964).

On the impact of the *Aufklärung* and the Enlightenment, with extensive bibliographical references, see M. Raeff, "Les Slaves, les

Allemands et les 'Lumières,' " *Revue canadienne d'études slaves* I, 4 (Hiver 1967), 521–51. On Russian philosophy, the most searching and original work is G. Florovsky, *Puti russkogo bogosloviia* (Paris, 1936); the most convenient and comprehensive survey is that of V. V. Zenkovsky, *A History of Russian Philosophy,* 2 vols. (London-New York, 1953). For Russian Masonry, there is now available a well-nigh complete bibliography, *La Franc-maçonnerie en Russie,* bibliography prepared by Paul Bourychkine, completed and updated by Tatiana Bakounine (Paris-The Hague, 1967), to which may be added the unpublished workmanlike dissertations of In-Ho Ryu (Harvard University, 1967), and G. H. McArthur (University of Rochester, 1968).

Radishchev's *cri de coeur, Journey from St. Petersburg to Moscow,* has been translated by L. Wiener and edited by R. Thaler (Harvard University, 1958). The best analytical study of his thought is by Allen McConnell, *A Russian Philosophe: Alexander Radishchev, 1749–1802* (The Hague, 1964). On the followers of Radishchev and the next generation of the Russian intelligentsia, see the review article by M. Raeff, "Filling the Gap Between Radishchev and the Decembrists," *Slavic Review,* XXVI, 3 (September 1967), 395–413. A most interesting discussion of Russian political thought in the early decades of the nineteenth century is in Leonard Schapiro, *Rationalism and Nationalism in Russian Nineteenth-century Political Thought* (Yale University, 1967). The contribution of Karamzin to this aspect of Russian intellectual life is thoroughly analyzed (as an introduction to a translation of Karamzin's major political pamphlet) by R. Pipes, *Karamzin's Memoir on Ancient and Modern Russia* (Harvard University, 1959). Unfortunately, there is still no adequate treatment of the seminal influence of Karamzin in the realm of culture and history.

The literature on the Decembrists is immense. The two classical monographs—one prerevolutionary, the other Soviet—are: V. I. Semevsky, *Politicheskie i obshchestvennye idei Dekabristov* (St. Petersburg, 1909), and M. V. Nechkina, *Dvizhenie Dekabristov,* 2 vols. (Moscow, 1955). A selection of sources, with an interpretive introductory essay, may be found in M. Raeff, *The Decembrist Movement* (Englewood Cliffs, N.J., 1966).

Index